Feel To Heal

A Guide to Feeling, Healing, and Living from the Truth of Who You Are

By Sharyn Nichols

Feel to Heal
SHARYN NICHOLS

Hardcover ISBN: 978-1-997615-32-3
Paperback ISBN: 978-1-997615-31-6
EBook ISBN: 978-1-997615-30-9
Illustrated by Milica Jelenic
Edited by Kim Dietrich, www.kimdietrich.ca
ICN INC.
ICN Publishing | www.icn-publishing.com

ICN Publishing

About ICN Publishing

ICN Publishing brings conscious voices to the world through print. We champion an inclusive range of authors and provide an open, supportive press for thought leaders who are ready to share messages that inspire, educate, and empower. Our titles span business, personal growth, health, wellness, and beyond – all aimed at promoting greater consciousness and choice.

As part of Inspired Choices Network, ICN Publishing is home to the Podcast to Bookshelf program – a done-for-you publishing pathway for visionary entrepreneurs, coaches, and thought leaders who want to transform their podcast episodes into captivating, reader-ready books. Through strategic content mapping, theme development, and full editorial and publishing support, Podcast to Bookshelf helps hosts expand their reach, grow their authority, and preserve their unique voice in print.

Together, ICN Publishing and Podcast to Bookshelf ensure that conscious voices aren't just heard – they're remembered.

Dedication

For all my children – you are my greatest teachers, my deepest mirrors, and the living proof of love in motion. You've shown me that healing is not something we do once – it's something we live, together, every day.

For my husband – thank you for holding space for all that I am becoming, and for loving me through every version of myself. Your steady presence has been both anchor and wings.

For my parents – you gave me the roots to grow and the courage to bloom. Every lesson, every story, every truth has shaped the woman and mother I've become.

And for my friends and extended family – thank you for reminding me to laugh, to rest, and to keep my heart open. You've walked beside me through the dark and danced with me in the light.

To my clients – thank you for your courage to feel, for showing me that healing is not about perfection, but presence.

To my community – those who have shared tears, tea, and truth – your love lives in these pages.

And to Cher Lyn, whose *Heart of the Jewel* graces this cover and captures the very essence of what this book is about – remembering that within our cracks, our heartbreaks, and our unravelings lives the sacred light that has been there all along.

Your art has always felt like a conversation between worlds – spirit speaking through color, movement, and emotion. I was blessed to witness you paint *Moses* in Sedona, to stand beside you as you invited me to bless it. In that moment, I understood that art could be prayer – that creation itself is an act of healing.

Your work reminds me that beauty is not perfection, it's presence – and that what glows most brightly in us often comes from the places we've dared to break open. Thank you for channeling light into form, for holding the vibration of truth, and for allowing your creation to become part of mine.

Please check out more of her work at www.mysticartmedicine.com.

Table of Contents

"Sometimes the truth cracks you open before it sets you free."

Introduction:
The Feel to Heal Journey

Every healing journey begins with honesty – the kind that can feel tender or even uncomfortable at first. When you couple that honesty with compassion, the truth of what you find begins to soften. It can help if you see the act of facing your truth not as something that is meant to break you – but rather as something that's meant to open you, and help you grow into the next version of yourself.

When we allow ourselves to face what's real, we create space for freedom, and that's what *Feel to Heal* is all about – both the podcast, and now this book.

When I first began my podcast, I wasn't trying to create a program or a brand – I was answering something inside me that knew there had to be another way to heal. I had watched so many people – clients, friends, even myself – try to think our way out of pain, to stay busy instead of feeling, to keep functioning even when we were quietly falling apart.

What I wanted was a place where we could pause long enough to listen. My *Feel to Heal* podcast became that space: a conversation about what it really means to grow, to stop performing, and to finally feel safe being human.

The Heart of Healing and Self-Trust

Emotional healing isn't about fixing yourself; it's about remembering that you were never broken. True growth begins when you stop managing your feelings and start feeling them. That's not easy work – it asks for patience, compassion, and courage especially, because for most of us, feeling doesn't always feel safe.

We've been taught to hide what hurts, to label emotions as weakness, to stay strong instead of stay real. But the body knows the truth – it carries what the mind avoids. And when we face that truth, though it may feel like it's cracking us open, it's actually what sets us free.

You'll notice as you read that I return to one truth again and again throughout these pages: ***healing doesn't happen in the mind; it happens in the body.*** That's not a slogan – it's the core of everything I teach. You'll see it repeated in different ways because it's the thread that ties this whole book together.

We *think* our way into pain, but we *feel* our way into healing. Every chapter is another invitation to come back to that truth.

Healing happens when you let yourself be seen – first by yourself, and then by the world around you. And what I hope you'll also discover here is that self-trust grows in the smallest, simplest ways: one honest breath, one clear boundary, and one moment at a time of staying with yourself instead of abandoning what's true.

How to Move Through This Book

Each chapter of *Feel to Heal* was born from a real conversation – from the lived experiences, insights, and tools I've shared through my practice and podcast. They can be read in any order and opened wherever you most need support. There's no right way to move through this book; there's only your way. Read slowly, pause when something stirs, and let your body tell you when to rest and when to continue.

My invitation is simple: take what resonates and leave the rest. Feel what you feel, trust what you know, and allow these pages to meet you where you are. As you read, keep in mind that healing isn't a destination – it's a return to yourself. That's what it's all about really – coming back to yourself. As I like to say, *you might as well be you; everyone else is already taken.*

"I felt like a narcissist when I first started honoring my own needs, but I learned that being focused on self doesn't make me a narcissist – it makes me healthy."

Chapter 1:
The Selfish Myth: Reclaiming the Right to Put Yourself First

Let's talk about selfishness, and not the pop-psychology version, but the version that lives quietly inside so many of us. That internal whisper that flares up the moment we put ourselves first. That voice that asks, "Who do you think you are?"

Because for those of us who were raised to prioritize everyone else – to be the good daughter, the good friend, the good partner, the dependable one – the moment we pause to take care of ourselves, it doesn't feel empowering. It feels wrong. It feels heavy. It feels like guilt.

But here's the truth: honoring your needs does not make you selfish. Taking care of yourself does not make you narcissistic. Saying no, resting, protecting your energy – none of that is a character flaw. In fact, it's the foundation of healing.

What I want to offer you in this chapter is a reframe. A new way of looking at selfishness, not as a shameful label, but as a doorway to self-respect. Because if you've ever been called selfish – or if you've ever called yourself that for simply wanting something – it's time to take another look.

The First Time You Were Called Selfish

Let's go back to the beginning. Try to remember: when was the first time someone called you selfish? For most of us, it was when we were very young. Toddlers, even. At that age, we're supposed to be egocentric – it's literally how our brains develop. We don't have the executive reasoning skills to understand other people's needs or experiences yet. We're wired to see the world through our own eyes first.

And then someone older, someone whose brain *was* fully formed, called us 'selfish.' And even if they didn't mean it to sting, that's how it landed, and it planted a seed. And that seed grew into something many of us still carry: the belief that our own needs are a burden. But that way of thinking, that we should always put others first, is just plain wrong.

We don't just carry this into adulthood. We end up building our identities around it. We end up trying to prove that we are good enough. And it's no wonder. We live in a culture that rewards over-functioning, that praises burnout, and that defines worth according to productivity and self-sacrifice. We're taught to give, and give, and give... until we have nothing left – and then to feel guilty for needing a break.

But let me ask you this: if you don't take care of yourself, who will?

The Guilt That Follows Rest

Let's get really honest: how do you feel when you say no? When you take a break, skip a call, cancel plans, or just go for a walk alone... do you feel rested – or do you feel guilty? The guilt so many of us feel doesn't come from our truth. It comes from conditioning. It's the echo of all those moments when someone told you, either directly or indirectly, that your needs were too much. That your desires were inconvenient. That your 'no' was unkind.

But here's what I know to be true: taking care of yourself is not an act of selfishness. It's an act of self-preservation. Even during COVID – remember? – taking care of yourself became the very thing that protected others. Staying home, wearing a mask, and saying 'no' to gatherings. Yes, that was self-care, but it was also community care. And it reminded us that when we care for ourselves, we're better able to care for everyone else.

The same is true now. It's not selfish to rest. It's not selfish to say, "I need time." It's not selfish to ask yourself, "What do I want?" That's not narcissism. That's not being selfish. That's healing.

Redefining the Spectrum

We tend to see selfishness and selflessness as opposites. But they're not. They're part of the same spectrum. And every one of us lives somewhere on that line, shifting back and forth depending on what season we're in, what we've been taught, and how safe we feel to be honest.

There are moments when you *need* to think of yourself first. When you need to say no, cancel plans, turn inward, and rest. And there are also moments when your empathy kicks in and you stretch – when you support a friend even though you're tired or when you show up for someone because it matters. Both are valid. Both are human.

The trouble comes when we get stuck at the far ends of the spectrum. When we *always* put others first, we disappear. We become shells. We get resentful. And when we *only* think of ourselves – without awareness or compassion – we lose connection. We lose community.

There's so much space in the middle. There's space to breathe. To choose. To course-correct. To ask yourself: "Where am I today? What do I need right now?"

There is room for boundaries, for care, and for truth.

We don't talk enough about how healing it is to simply say: "This is what I need." Not in a loud, demanding way. But in a quiet, grounded way. A way that says: "I've checked in. I'm listening to myself. And this is my truth."

And yes – when you first start doing this, it might feel uncomfortable. You might feel guilty. You might hear that old echo: "You're being selfish." But what you're actually doing is *rebalancing*. You're adjusting the weight that's been tipped too far in one direction for too long. You're practicing being in alignment. You're coming home to yourself.

Letting Go of the Martyr Role

I see this play out so often – especially with women. You ask for something: "Can you watch the kids for a couple of hours?" But before the other person can even respond, you say: "Oh, never mind. I'll figure it out."

That's not selfless. That's martyrdom. And it creates a lose-lose situation because you don't get the support you need and the other person doesn't get a chance to show up for you. And then everyone walks away a little more depleted.

Instead, what if you said, "I need help. And I want this to be a win-win. If you say yes, how can I support you in return? Maybe you were planning to go food shopping? Great – I can pick up dinner, and we can make this work for both of us." That's not selfish. That's collaboration.

It's also an acknowledgment that we are not meant to do life alone. We're not meant to carry everything by ourselves. Even me – sitting down to record my podcasts – I couldn't do it without a whole team of people supporting me.

Literally and energetically. And if I let guilt or pride or the fear of being "too much" get in the way of asking for help, I wouldn't be here. I wouldn't be using my voice. I wouldn't be doing what I love.

Boundaries Are Not Walls

Now let's talk about boundaries – because this is where so many of us get tangled up. Especially those of us who've been taught to say yes before we even check in with ourselves.

Somewhere along the way, we were taught that saying 'no' is rude, that having preferences makes us difficult. Or, that expressing our limits is unkind – or worse, selfish. That a "good person" is someone who's always available, always agreeable, always flexible. But that's just more of the same conditioning – and it's exhausting.

Boundaries are not walls. They're not punishments. They're not ultimatums. Boundaries are not about pushing people away. They are about *letting people in* – in a way that feels safe, respectful, and aligned. A true boundary says: "Here's what works for me. And I trust you enough to be honest about it."

Boundaries help us stay in right relationship with ourselves. They help us protect our energy, our time, and our nervous systems. And they help us build trust – because when you say yes, people know you mean it. And when you say no, people can believe you. That's what creates safety.

Without boundaries, everything becomes a guessing game. We make many assumptions and expect people to read our minds. We hope they'll just "know" what we need. And when they don't – when they get it wrong – we feel hurt, disappointed, maybe even resentful. That's not honesty – it's a setup.

Boundaries don't create distance – they create clarity. They help us create *win-win* situations, where everyone involved gets to make an empowered choice.

And here's the key difference: Setting a boundary is *not* manipulation. Manipulation is when you ask for something, but only one answer is acceptable. When you push for a yes and don't allow space for a no. When your request becomes a demand, or your yes comes with resentment attached.

A healthy boundary allows for a full response. It gives everyone room to say what's true for them. And that kind of honesty is what real connection is built on. When someone sets a boundary with you – when they say, "No, I can't help with that today" – that's not a rejection. That's information. That's them honoring themselves, and inviting you to do the same. And when you set a boundary – when you say, "No, I don't have capacity for that right now" – you're not being selfish. You're being wise. You're trusting that your truth matters too.

Boundaries protect peace. They protect energy. They protect relationships. Not from conflict – but from the dishonesty, resentment, and silent expectations that erode trust over time.

And yes – it can feel hard at first. Especially if you're not used to it. Especially if people are used to you being "the easy one." But the more you practice, the more you'll notice how grounding it is to be clear. How freeing it is to stop performing. How truly loving it is to be real.

Reparenting the Little You

When you care for yourself – when you rest, when you say no, when you step back from doing all the things for all the people – you're not just protecting your energy in the present; you're healing something from the past. You're unwinding the shame you've been carrying, maybe without even realizing it. You're interrupting the pattern that says everyone else comes first – and you're gently replacing it with a new truth.

You're showing the younger version of you – the one who was told she was too much, too emotional, too needy – that she's allowed to exist. That her needs matter. That she doesn't have to justify every choice, or apologize for taking up space. You're showing her she doesn't have to earn rest.

You're reparenting her. And that's powerful. That's how the healing really begins – not by fixing something, but by offering the kind of care you never received in the moment it was most needed. Because self-care, when you really practice it, is not performative. It's not a curated morning routine or a checklist of bubble baths and green smoothies, (unless those things truly nourish you.) It's not something you 'do' to get it right or prove your worth.

It's about listening. Honoring. Noticing when something feels off and giving yourself permission to pause. It's about asking, "What do I need right now?" and trusting the answer – even if it's inconvenient, even if no one else understands, and even if it feels unfamiliar.

Self-care is a radical act of truth-telling. And sometimes that truth is quiet. Sometimes that truth says, "Not today." Or "That's enough." Or even just, "I matter too."

You Are Not a Narcissist

Let's clear this up once and for all: there is a big difference between being self-aware and being self-absorbed. Between self-honoring and self-aggrandizing. Between taking responsibility for your own energy and believing the world revolves around you.

Narcissistic Personality Disorder is a clinical diagnosis, and I say this not just as a therapist, but as someone who's walked beside people through the confusion and pain of these dynamics. It's not a casual label to throw at someone who simply took a day off or posted a photo of themselves smiling.

True narcissism is not just about confidence or visibility. It's defined by a pervasive pattern of grandiosity, entitlement, manipulative behavior, and most notably, a profound lack of empathy. Narcissists tend to be preoccupied with admiration, control, and image. They often can't tolerate criticism, and they struggle – sometimes completely refuse – to take accountability for how their behavior impacts others.

And while someone might display narcissistic *traits* now and then (we all have moments where we're caught up in ourselves), that does not mean they meet the clinical threshold for Narcissistic Personality Disorder. For that diagnosis to apply, the behavior has to be chronic, extreme, and impairing across multiple areas of life. Most people don't even come close.

So let's be clear: That's *not* what we're talking about here. We're not talking about manipulation. We're not talking about arrogance. We're not talking about a lack of empathy.

We're talking about you learning how to take care of yourself, about you finally saying 'no' without over-explaining. We're talking about you setting boundaries, asking for what you need, and choosing to stop abandoning yourself in the name of being "good."

We're talking about unlearning over-functioning, stepping out of the performance, and letting go of the need to prove your worth through exhaustion.

That is *healing*. That is *health* – not narcissism.

And yes – there may be people who don't understand that, people who benefited from your old patterns, who feel unsettled when you stop people-pleasing. You may be called selfish. You may be misunderstood. But that doesn't mean you're doing something wrong.

If someone withdraws because you expressed a need, that's information. If someone pushes back when you set a boundary, that's information. If someone calls you selfish just because you're finally tending to your own wellbeing, that's information.

It's not a cue to shrink. It's not a cue to apologize for growing. It's a cue to check in with yourself – and to hold your ground, gently but firmly. Because you know who you are. You know your intention. And you know the difference between being self-centered, and finally being centered in/on yourself.

A Final Reflection

I'll leave you with this: You can't pour from an empty cup. You can't keep giving when you've abandoned yourself. And you certainly can't show up in truth if you're constantly editing yourself to make others comfortable.

So where are you on the spectrum? Are you still carrying the fear of being called selfish? Are you still shrinking your needs to avoid conflict? Are you still overextending, hoping someone will validate you? Maybe today is the day you begin to lay that down?

Because selfish isn't always bad. Sometimes, it's the first step toward self-trust, toward self-respect, and toward healing. You matter. Your needs matter. Your truth matters. And putting yourself first may just be the most generous thing you can do.

"When I assumed, I disconnected – not just from others, but from myself."

Chapter 2: Assumptions, Projections, and the Stories We Tell Ourselves

It happens in a breath. Someone doesn't text back right away. A tone shifts. A look lingers just a little too long, and before you even realize it, your mind has written a whole story about what it means. We do it so quickly – filling in gaps, layering old experiences onto new moments – that it feels automatic. And in many ways, it is, because our mind is trying to make sense of what feels uncertain. But when we assume, we disconnect – not just from the other person, but from ourselves.

I know this one well. I can trace countless moments where my mind leapt in to "protect" me by analyzing, interpreting, or assigning meaning. It always felt safer to know something, even if what I "knew" wasn't true. But the more I stayed in my head, the more I drifted from what was real – the sensations in my body, the truth of the moment, and the person standing right in front of me.

That's the thing about assumptions: they pretend to offer us safety, but they actually create separation. The mind tells a story so we don't have to feel the discomfort of not knowing. But healing doesn't happen in the mind – it happens in the body. And the body always knows the difference between story and truth.

So this chapter isn't about judging the mind for doing what it's learned to do – it's about learning to notice that pattern, learning to pause before the story becomes a fact, and anchoring in the body, where presence and truth still live.

When you start to catch yourself mid-assumption, don't rush to correct it. Just notice. Breathe. Ask quietly, *"What am I making this mean?"* Often that's all it takes to interrupt the spiral – not because you've figured anything out, but because you've remembered to anchor in yourself.

When a Tone Becomes a Story

I remember a time when someone I loved sounded distant on the phone. Their voice was flat, their tone almost lifeless. Before we even hung up, my stomach had already started to tighten. *What did I do? Did I say something wrong?* Within minutes, I was scrolling through my mental files, searching for clues, replaying conversations, and furiously trying to locate the moment where things must have gone sideways.

Hours later, I learned they were just exhausted. Nothing more. No hidden meaning, no secret resentment – just a human being who'd had a long day. And I realized how quickly my own fear had filled the space where curiosity could have lived.

This is what the mind does when it's unsure. It creates certainty, even if that certainty hurts. It assigns tone, intention, and motive to keep you from feeling the raw ache of ambiguity. But every time we do that, we move a little farther away from connection – not only with the other person, but with ourselves.

When I work with clients, I see this pattern over and over again. A partner sighs and the other withdraws. A friend takes a little longer to reply, and suddenly there's a whole inner courtroom deciding what it means. We begin to respond to our assumptions rather than to what's actually happening.

One of the most healing things we can do in those moments is to slow down. To soften enough to say, *"I noticed you sounded quiet earlier – are you okay?"* or *"I might be misunderstanding – can you tell me what you meant?"* Asking doesn't make you needy. It makes you honest.

When I assumed, I disconnected. But the times when I asked, I reconnected – every single time.

The Stories We See Through

It's amazing how easily we can confuse what's happening inside of us with what's happening around us. We look at someone's face, hear a tone, or sense a shift, and before we know it, we've filled in the blanks. Our mind says, *"I know what this means."* We assume that everyone thinks how we think, feels as we feel, and judges the way we judge.

But that isn't truth – it's interpretation. It's the story we tell when we're unsure. When we've been hurt, our nervous system learns to scan for danger. So when something feels even a little familiar, we react as if it's happening again. We see through old lenses, the ones that were shaped by earlier experiences, and it can make the present moment feel distorted.

I've watched this play out so many times – in clients, in relationships, and in myself. Someone says a few words and I'm already halfway down the road of what I think they mean. But what I've learned is that those moments are invitations. They're a chance to pause, breathe, and ask, *"What's actually here right now?"*

That's what awareness looks like. It's not about blaming yourself for misunderstanding. It's about recognizing when your past is coloring the present, and choosing to stay curious instead of certain. You don't have to fix it, just notice it. Each time you do, you loosen the story's hold a little more – and in that space, truth has room to surface.

When Overthinking Feels Protective

Overthinking often masquerades as responsibility. It tells you that if you analyze hard enough, replay every detail, predict every outcome, you'll finally be safe. But what it really does is keep you trapped in motion without movement – running laps around the same worry until your body forgets how to rest.

I used to believe that if I could just think my way through every possible scenario, I could avoid pain. But pain doesn't get smaller through analysis; it gets louder. When we stay in our heads, we bypass the very place where healing can happen.

I once had a client who spent a whole day spiraling because early in the day his wife said, "We need to talk tonight." He imagined every possible reason – all of them catastrophic. By the time they finally sat down together, he was full of dread. And what did she want to talk about? Remodeling the guest bathroom – that was it!

His nervous system wasn't trying to hurt him. It was trying to protect him. But protection built on fear ends up feeling like punishment. When the mind races ahead, the body tightens to keep up – and suddenly we're living in imagined futures instead of the moment we're actually in.

When that happens, place a hand on your heart. Breathe. Ask yourself, *"What do I know for sure right now?"*

That question grounds you in the present. And remember, you don't have to solve what hasn't happened. You just need to be here, now.

The Road Trip Back to Each Other

We can think about relationships a little like a road trip. You start out aligned, talking, laughing, and both headed in the same direction. Then something shifts – a misunderstanding, a misread tone – and suddenly the scenery looks unfamiliar. But instead of pulling over, we so often press harder on the gas. We want to get through the discomfort quickly.

The problem is, assumptions take you further off course. Every time you don't ask a question for clarification, the gap widens. And before long, you're both staring out opposite windows, wondering how you ended up so far apart.

If you notice that happening, it's okay to stop. Pull over. Take a breath. Ask for directions together. Simple phrases like, *"Can we pause? I think we might have gotten off track,"* can reset an entire conversation. It's not about being right; it's about finding your way back to the same road.

You can use this practice in any of your relationships – with friends, with family, with colleagues – because when we take that pause and check the map together, there's a visible softening. Our defenses drop. The body relaxes. And suddenly we remember that we're on the same team.

Healing isn't about never getting lost. It's about knowing how to return to the truth of ourselves.

The Council of Three

When my thoughts start spinning, I return to something I call the *council of three*: mind, body, and soul. The mind has a seat at the table – it's sharp, quick, analytical – but it doesn't get to lead. The body sits next to it, holding all the wisdom of experience. And at the head of the table is the soul, quiet but clear, guiding the conversation back toward truth.

When I practice this, I close my eyes and imagine each one speaking in turn. I let the mind say what it needs – all its fears and plans and details. I say thank you. Then I listen to the body: Where am I holding tension? What sensations want my attention? Finally, I turn to the soul and ask, *"What is my next right step?"*

This isn't about silencing your thoughts. It's about bringing them back into relationship with the rest of you. When the mind and body remember that the soul is driving, the spiral slows. You start to feel anchored again – connected to yourself instead of lost in the noise.

You can't think your way to peace. You can only feel your way there.

Back to the Body

Our assumptions have physical signatures. Maybe your chest tightens. Maybe your jaw clenches. Maybe your shoulders rise just enough that you stop breathing deeply. These are all cues that something inside you needs attention, and healing happens when we start to follow those cues instead of ignoring them.

So, take a breath, feel your feet on the ground, notice the texture of the air against your skin. When you come back into your body like this, that's where the stories and assumptions can begin to loosen. That's where you can start to see that what felt like absolute truth might just be a familiar pattern playing out again.

You could even imagine pressing "pause" on a thought and then turning the volume down so you can notice what the body is saying underneath. Often it's something simple like, *"I'm scared,"* or *"I need reassurance."* When you can name what's really there, compassion can finally enter the room.

You're not broken for having these reactions. They're part of how your nervous system learned to survive. And every time you meet them with curiosity instead of criticism, you build trust with yourself. That's what healing is – a thousand small returns to the body, over and over again – because the body has the answers. Your mind was never meant to run your life – it was meant to reflect it. Your body holds the truth; your mind just tries to make sense of it.

Practicing Assumption Hygiene

If you want to see how often assumptions sneak in, try tracking them for a week. Write them down as they happen – the little stories, not just the big ones. "She didn't say hi, she must be mad." "He didn't answer, he must not care." Seeing them in writing helps you recognize how your mind fills silence with fear.

Once you spot one, try to avoid going into the 'why'. Instead, take a breath, and focus on the 'what' – label it gently: *"That's a story."* Then ask for clarity if you need it, and if it's safe to do so. You might say, *"The story I'm telling myself is that you're upset – is that true?"* or *"I'm realizing I might have assumed something; can we check in?" or "I am making an assumption, please correct me if I am wrong."*

Each time you do this, you're practicing something far more powerful than positive thinking – you're practicing presence. You're reminding your nervous system that truth lives in real-time connection, not imagined conclusions.

And if you can, extend that same curiosity toward yourself. Ask, *"What story am I telling about me?"* Because often, the harshest assumptions are the ones we hold about our own worth.

When "Knowing" Feels Safer Than Asking

So many of us grew up believing that being easy – agreeable, low-maintenance, undemanding – was how we earned love. We learned to fill in blanks quietly, to pretend we understood, to avoid asking too many questions. It made us feel safe because it kept the peace. And over time, that kind of knowing became heavy. It cost us authenticity.

I've had to unlearn that pattern myself. There's still a small part of me that wants to prove I'm not too much, not too sensitive, not too demanding. But I've realized that honest questions create more safety than silence ever did.

When something feels unclear, start small. Ground yourself – two breaths, feet on the floor – and then speak from truth. *"The story I'm telling myself is... Is that accurate?"* or *"I might have misread that – can you tell me what you meant?"* It's a simple practice, but one that requires bravery, and in the end, builds trust.

You don't have to get it perfect. You'll forget. You'll assume again. You'll catch yourself halfway through a spiral and have to start over. That's okay. Healing isn't a straight line. It's not one and done. Every time you choose curiosity over certainty, you're re-teaching your body what safety actually feels like.

A Closing Reflection

Assumptions will always try to pull you away from presence. That's just how the mind works – scanning, sorting, searching for safety. But you are not your mind. You are the awareness beneath it, the breath that can pause and say, *"Wait – what's actually true right now?"*

When we stay in our moments of false belief, we feel less. Resisting assumptions, on the other hand, leads us to enhanced communications, better conversations, and improved friendships. When we allow ourselves to feel less guarded, we allow others in – and that kind of vulnerability is sexy.

You can't think your way through this work. You have to feel it. Stay with the sensations, stay with the breath, stay with the conversation even when it feels uncomfortable. Because that's where healing begins – in the moments you choose connection over protection, truth over story, and presence over performance.

You're not broken – within you lies the power to rewrite all those limiting stories you've been telling yourself for so long. You are capable of change – and it will happen one pause, one breath, and one honest question at a time.

"It's okay to be afraid. And it's not okay to
let fear drive the bus.
Let fear be your compass."

Chapter 3: Fear Is Not a Stop Sign

We all know fear. It's that flutter in your chest when you're about to speak the truth, the knot in your stomach when you're about to make a change, the thought that whispers, *what if I can't handle this?* For a long time, I thought fear meant something was wrong with me – that I wasn't confident enough or healthy enough – that I hadn't done enough healing. What I've learned, though, is that fear is part of being human. It's the body's way of saying, "Something here matters."

Fear used to run my life in quiet, but convincing ways. I didn't call it fear back then – I called it staying busy, being productive, or getting things just right. I thought if I kept everything together, I'd feel safe. But underneath all that desire for control was the same trembling energy: I didn't want to fail. I didn't want to disappoint anyone. I didn't want to feel what I didn't yet know how to face.

The truth is, fear isn't something to eliminate. It's something to understand. It's the protector that tries to keep us from getting hurt again. But when we let it make the decisions, it keeps us from growing. Healing begins when we can feel the fear without letting it drive. We start to heal when we can notice what's happening in our body – the tension, the holding, the breath we forget to take – and stay with it long enough to remember that we are safe in this moment.

Fear doesn't mean stop – it means pay attention. It means *slow down* enough to hear what your body's trying to tell you, instead of rushing to fix it.

When Fear Runs the Show

Fear is sneaky too. It wears a lot of different disguises – perfectionism, control, avoidance, even rushing. It tells you to move faster so you won't feel. It piles on expectations so you won't risk. It convinces you that if you can just get it *right*, you'll finally be safe.

I used to live that way. The busier I was, the more in control I felt – until my body started to tell the truth I didn't want to hear – exhaustion, headaches, and a nervous system locked on high alert. My mind kept saying, "Push through," but my body whispered, "Please stop." Fear had become my operating system, and I didn't even know it.

Here's the truth: fear can keep us anywhere but the present. It loops you into the future – *What if I fail? What if I look foolish?* – or drags you back into old pain. It says, *Don't try. Don't rest. Don't ask.* Stay small and you won't get hurt. And yet, that not-trying hurts too.

The quieter voice underneath – the one that you hear in the shower, before sleep, or in a friend's kindness – that voice is different. It's the one that says things like, *You're doing a great job. You are enough. Breathe. Let's begin again.* When you listen for that voice, you'll find your fear begin to loosen. You'll find yourself back in your body. And that's where you remember you have choice about what to do next.

Protector and Blocker

Fear is both protector and blocker. The mind is brilliant at keeping us safe – sometimes too brilliant. It's constantly scanning for danger, asking, *What could go wrong?* That instinct comes from love. It's your nervous system trying to protect you from the pain you've already known. The problem is that it doesn't always recognize the difference between real danger and emotional growth. It reacts the same way whether you're standing at a cliff's edge or simply stepping towards something new.

I've seen this so many times – in my own life and with clients. The moment you start to move toward change, the alarms go off. Your heart races, your breath shortens, your shoulders tighten, and your mind begins to warn, *Don't say that. Don't do that. You'll fail. You'll lose everything you've built.* That isn't truth; it's the ego doing its job, trying to keep you inside the lines of what feels familiar.

Fear doesn't just stop us from danger – it stops us from expansion. It tries to prevent what's called ego death – an experience in which you lose yourself – that moment when an old story or identity starts to dissolve. The ego says, *If you let go of being the one who holds it all together, who will you be?* It feels like death, but it's really rebirth. The irony is that fear's job is to save your life, but most of the time it's only saving your identity – the outdated version of who you used to be.

That's why I remind people that fear is "false evidence appearing real." It looks convincing, and it sounds like wisdom, but it's really saying, *Stay safe. Play small.* But when you pause long enough to breathe and ask, *Am I actually in danger right now?*, the truth begins to reveal itself. What's underneath fear is often vulnerability, anticipation, or even the energy of possibility.

When you move from fear into grounded power, you stop fighting yourself. You start listening. You say, *I see you, fear. I know you're trying to protect me. But I've got it from here.* That simple acknowledgment changes everything. The body settles, the breath deepens, and the mind loosens its grip. You begin to act from awareness instead of reactivity – one grounded breath, one honest conversation, and one clear choice at a time.

Fear, Perfectionism, and the Pace That Keeps You Numb

Perfectionism is fear's favorite disguise. It looks polished, driven, capable – but underneath, it's just scared. Scared of being seen as not enough. Scared of failing. Scared of not having it all together. For a long time, that was me.

When I started the podcast, I thought I had to get it right from day one. I really did. I thought I should already know what I was doing – that I should show up sounding like an expert, perfectly polished, no stumbles, no second takes. But I didn't – I got flustered, I got emotional, I was crying at points and afterwards I felt like I failed miserably. I remember thinking, I don't know what I'm doing. I thought I was prepared. I was 'should-ing' all over myself – I should have it figured out, I should be confident, I should never sound so unsure.

That's the trap of perfectionism – it keeps you moving fast so you don't have to feel. It tells you if you can just make it flawless, you'll finally be safe. But the truth is, all that proving keeps you numb. It pulls you out of your body and away from what's real.

Eventually, I realized the fear underneath all that control wasn't about the podcast at all. It was about being seen. I wanted to look like I had it all together because I thought that was the only way people would listen. But it turns out, the moments when I stumbled – the moments I cried through an episode or lost my words – those were the moments people connected with the most.

Now, I see failure differently. I see it as an opportunity. It's not shameful or horrible – it's information. It's feedback. It's part of the process. When I look back on those early episodes, I can smile because they were exactly what they needed to be. They were honest and human – just like me.

And that's what I want for you too – to let go of the 'shoulds.' They're loud, and they're not wisdom. When you soften your jaw, drop your shoulders, and take one real breath, you come back to what is – back to yourself. And remember not to get frustrated with yourself, because this won't be a one and done. As with all personal growth, you'll practice this again and again – breath by breath, choice by choice. And when you find yourself in that place, remember, that's not a failure; that's the path.

Fear vs. Actual Danger

Your nervous system is designed to scan for danger. Sometimes it gets it right; sometimes it's reacting to old echoes and unknowns. Part of healing is learning the difference.

Danger asks for immediate protective action. Fear asks for curiosity and care. When your body tenses and your mind spins, pause. Ask: *Am I safe right now? What is this feeling asking me to tend? Can I slow down enough to listen?* The answer might be a boundary, a glass of water, a walk around the block, or a call to a friend. It might be rest, or it might be, *Not today.* All of those are allowed and welcomed.

You don't have to bulldoze yourself to prove you're brave. Courage isn't white-knuckling through; it's choosing what's true, with your feet on the ground. The difference between danger and fear is the difference between contraction and awareness. One tightens; the other invites you to breathe.

What Sits Under Fear

Very often, fear is the top layer. Underneath, there's grief for what was lost, shame for what you made it mean, tenderness you didn't feel safe to show. Fear says, *Don't go there. It'll be too much.* But the body carries what the mind avoids – in the tight throat, the shallow breath, or the ache in the chest that doesn't go away.

Feeling is not punishment; it's the way through. We have to feel it to heal it. We have to sit with the wave and let it crest. I like to walk through a meditation on this where you just notice your breath as you inhale and exhale. Inhale compassion and grace and exhale loudly all the thoughts that are constricting you. Let go and let yourself be soothed by the rhythm of your own breath.

Breathe in compassion, breathe out guilt and perfection. Breathe in forgiveness, breathe out the lies of not-enough. When you stay with it – gently, honestly – it starts to shift those fears and those 'shoulds.' Yes, it takes courage to face what hides beneath fear. But when you do, you discover that what looked like weakness is actually the doorway to strength.

My Own "Stop Sign": Failing and Beginning Again

If you've listened to the my podcast, you know I've failed. Colossally, sometimes. I failed out of college. I was told I wasn't smart enough, that maybe I should rethink my path. But something in me refused to let fear be the final word. I took summer classes, raised my GPA, finished my business degree, and later earned my master's with honors. The fear in that season was loud – the shame was louder – but the truth was loudest: my worth was never measured by a number.

That experience taught me what I now tell clients: failure is an event, not an identity. You are not a failure because something failed. You tried. You learned. You changed. Fear wanted me to quit; courage asked me to begin again.

When you think about all the people who had failed before they succeeded – actors, inventors, leaders, artists – you end up with a very long list of names. Walt Disney, Elvis Presley, Colonel Sanders – imagine if they had all given up at the first failure, or even the hundredth? When you think about it, it's really humbling to remember that success stories are built on thousands of "not yets." And when we can redefine failure as feedback for ourselves, that's when fear loses its power, and we start to live from curiosity instead of comparison.

Gentle Tools for When Fear Rises

Start with your breath. Receive a breath. Inhale… hold… exhale… hold out. Simple counts. Feel your feet on the floor. Name five things you see, four you feel, three you hear. This is how you come back to your body when your mind is sprinting ahead.

Shift from force to power. Force is the pushing, proving, perfecting. Power is rooted presence. It's saying, *I'm safe to be here*. It's letting your energy expand instead of contract. Sometimes that means one courageous text – "I need help." Sometimes it's a boundary – "I don't have capacity today." Sometimes it's a pivot – the smallest shift that moves you out of the old loop and into truth. Each small act says, *I'm steering now*.

Keep a few truths close: you can't think your way through it; healing doesn't happen in the mind – it happens in the body. Fear is information, not identity. Stay with it. Stay gentle.

When fear tells you you're the only one, remember: everyone fails spectacularly at least once. What matters is what you make of it. I love the stories of people who were cut, rejected, booed off stage, told "no" a thousand times – and showed up again. Not to prove anything to the world, but to stay true to themselves.

Let their courage echo in your bones. Not as pressure to do more, but as permission to keep going in the way that's right for you. We aren't meant to do this alone. Ask for support. Receive it. Offer it. That's power – not power over, but power for – the kind that expands from the inside out.

A Closing Reflection

Fear will visit. Let it. Acknowledge it. Thank it for trying to keep you safe. Then take a breath, feel your feet, and choose your next honest step – not the perfect one, the true one.

And then think about this – where is fear trying to drive your bus? What is one gentle action that says, *I'm steering now*? Put your hand on your heart. Whisper it. And then – softly, steadily – go. Feel it to heal it. Stay with it, and keep on going.

“Forgiveness isn’t saying it was okay.
It’s saying I’m okay.”

Chapter 4: Forgiveness Isn't What You Think It Is

For a long time I believed that forgiveness meant I had to let someone off the hook. I thought if I forgave them, I was saying what they did was acceptable. So I held on – tight, and I replayed the moments, the conversations, and all the hurts. Maybe on some level I believed that if I stayed angry enough, I could somehow make it right. What I didn't realize was that I was keeping myself bound to the very thing I wanted freedom from. That's the tricky part about resentment: it feels powerful at first, like armor, but over time it becomes a cage.

Forgiveness, as I've come to see it, isn't about the other person at all. It's about me reclaiming my energy and saying, "I'm done carrying this." It's the release that happens when you realize your nervous system is tired of being in defense mode and your body is exhausted from holding the same pain. Forgiveness isn't quick or clean – it's a process you return to each time the sting resurfaces, a practice of letting your body unclench a little more each time.

Holding on to anger almost felt productive at one point – as if my pain was proof that I was right. But healing doesn't happen in the mind; it happens in the body. The longer I clung to the narrative, the heavier it felt. I could feel it in my chest, my shoulders, even my breath. But the moment I began to soften wasn't when I decided to forget; it was when I decided to stop fighting my own healing.

When I finally said, "I don't have to make this okay to be okay," something shifted. The grip loosened. Forgiveness wasn't about rewriting history; it was about letting something go within myself.

The Moment That Changed Everything

I remember watching Oprah tell a story that completely reframed forgiveness for me. She talked about how she was still angry at someone who had hurt her. This person had apologized and gone on with their life, humming along, seemingly unaffected. Meanwhile, Oprah was still fuming. She realized that while she was stuck in the loop of anger, the other person had moved on. They were free, and she was alone in continuing to carry the weight.

I could feel where I was still doing the same thing – holding on long after the moment had passed. Forgiveness, I realized, was about reclaiming my own peace. It was about deciding that I didn't want to keep giving my energy to something that wasn't happening anymore. That clarity didn't mean the pain vanished, but it did mean I could finally stop feeding it.

Forgiveness is for you – the one who's been carrying the story in your body long after it stopped being written.

When the Old Definition Stops Working

For a long time, I believed forgiveness required that moment of reconciliation where two people meeting in mutual understanding, clearing the air, moving forward together. But what happens when that moment never comes? What if the other person never takes responsibility or even sees what they've done? For years, that question kept me spinning. I told myself that if they didn't apologize, I couldn't forgive. And if I couldn't forgive, I couldn't move on. My entire sense of peace was tied to their willingness to change.

What I learned, slowly and painfully, is that waiting for someone else to make it right keeps you stuck in the same emotional loop. Sometimes forgiveness begins when you realize you may never hear the words you think you need. The closure has to come from inside you. It's not about rewriting the story – it's about reclaiming your place in it.

The body knows when it's ready. Sometimes that readiness looks like exhaustion, when you finally say, "I can't keep carrying this anymore." That's when the old definition loses its grip. Forgiveness stops being a performance of virtue and becomes a quiet act of self-liberation. It's not loud. It's not dramatic. It's just the steady release of what's been weighing you down.

Choosing Freedom Over Return

One of the hardest lessons for me – and for so many of the clients I've sat with – is understanding that you can forgive someone without ever going back. The relationship doesn't have to be resurrected for forgiveness to be real. I used to think walking away meant I hadn't forgiven enough, that if I were truly healed, I'd be able to stay. But staying isn't always love. Sometimes it's self-betrayal.

You can hold compassion for someone and still protect your boundaries. You can wish them peace and still choose distance. When I finally began to see forgiveness as an internal process rather than a relational one, I could breathe again. Forgiveness was me taking my power back from the dynamic – no longer needing to be understood or validated to be free.

That shift didn't happen overnight. There were moments when I caught myself testing the boundary, checking whether I "should" reach out, wondering if silence made me cold. But forgiveness isn't measured by contact; it's measured by peace. Every time I chose not to re-enter a painful cycle, my body thanked me. The release came in waves – sometimes gentle, sometimes messy – but always leading me closer to myself.

Forgiveness, in its truest form, doesn't erase the past or reopen old doors. It honors the truth of what happened while choosing not to let it define who you become. That is freedom.

The Emotional Cost of Holding On

We don't always realize how much energy resentment consumes. The anger, the rumination, the quiet rehearsals of what we wish we'd said – all of it takes a toll. You think you're protecting yourself, but really you're keeping your body in a constant state of readiness, braced against a threat that no longer exists. Your nervous system doesn't know the difference between the memory and the moment. Every time you replay the hurt, your body tightens again. That's why forgiveness isn't an idea – it's a physiological release.

I remember a time when I was convinced I had let go, but then a small reminder – a scent, a song, a familiar phrase – would send me right back into the story. My chest would constrict. My breath would shorten. That was my body telling me there was still something I hadn't released – because remember, healing doesn't happen in the mind. It happens in the body. The work is to notice where the pain still lives, and to stay with it, and breathe through it, long enough for it to soften.

The cost of holding on is subtle but relentless. It seeps into how you speak to others, how you trust, how you rest.

When you carry old anger, it becomes the lens through which you see new experiences. You begin to expect disappointment, to anticipate betrayal. Forgiveness interrupts that pattern. It's not a denial of what happened; it's a declaration that you deserve to live unguarded again, and that, really, is the quiet miracle of forgiveness – it gives you back to yourself.

When the Pain Returns

There's a myth that once you've forgiven, the pain should never resurface. But emotions don't follow timelines. Sometimes forgiveness feels complete until something nudges the old wound – a conversation, a holiday, a dream – and suddenly it's raw again. That doesn't mean you've failed. It means you're human. Healing is cyclical. You may return to the same place many times, but each time you arrive with a little more awareness, a little more capacity to stay present with what arises.

When that happens, my practice is simple: pause, breathe, and remember that it's okay to feel it again. The body carries memory. It will bring forward what's ready to be released, and it may do so in layers. The invitation isn't to push it away, but to meet it with curiosity. What is this feeling asking for now? What part of me still needs to be witnessed?

I've learned that the return of pain can be a profound teacher. It shows you how far you've come, how much softer you've become with yourself. Early in my healing, I used to meet resurfacing pain with judgment – "I should be over this by now." Now I meet it with compassion – "Of course this still hurts." That shift changes everything.

Forgiveness isn't one grand act. It's the ongoing willingness to come back to yourself, over and over, without shame. The pain may visit again, but you no longer let it take up residence.

Forgiving Yourself

Self-forgiveness is often the hardest kind. You can understand, intellectually, that you did your best with what you knew at the time, but the mind still clings to the "if onlys." If only I'd spoken up sooner. If only I'd left earlier. If only I hadn't trusted them. Those thoughts become loops that keep you anchored to regret. They replay in the background, shaping how you see yourself.

There was a time when I couldn't even say the words "I forgive myself" without tears catching in my throat. The idea felt indulgent, almost wrong. But that was the same conditioning that kept me believing worth had to be earned. Forgiveness doesn't erase accountability – it invites compassion into it. When you can look at your younger self and say, “You were doing the best you could,” you begin to reclaim the pieces that shame pushed away.

The nervous system plays a role here too. The body remembers every moment you froze instead of spoke, every time you overrode intuition to stay safe. Self-forgiveness is the slow thawing of those moments. It’s letting the body know the threat has passed. You don’t need to keep punishing yourself to prove you’ve learned.

Forgiving yourself is not permission to repeat the past; it’s permission to move beyond it. It’s you saying, “I’m allowed to heal.” And when you do, the same grace you extend inward naturally begins to flow outward.

The Courage to Stay Soft

Forgiveness asks for softness in a world that rewards armor. It’s much easier to harden – to turn the hurt into a story of survival, to build identity around what you’ve endured. But true healing invites the opposite movement. It asks you to stay open-hearted in places where you once closed. It asks you to trust that vulnerability isn’t weakness; it’s wisdom.

There’s a line I return to often: “You can’t think your way through it.” You can analyze pain forever, but until you let yourself feel it, it won’t move. The mind wants control; the heart wants connection. Forgiveness is what bridges the two. It’s a softening that happens in the body, one breath at a time. Sometimes that softness feels terrifying. The old defenses whisper, "Don't do this. You'll get hurt again." But healing doesn't happen behind walls. It happens when you risk presence – when you sit with, and breathe through, those old hurts.

Choosing softness doesn't mean tolerating harm. It means you no longer need to lead with tension. You can meet the world with clear eyes and a steady heart, grounded in your own truth. That's a quiet kind of courage – the courage to be fully human, to feel it all, and to keep your heart open anyway.

Every time you stay soft instead of shutting down, you teach your body a new story: that safety doesn't live in control; it lives in presence. Forgiveness opens that door.

Returning to the Practice

Forgiveness isn't a milestone you cross and leave behind; it's a path you keep walking. Some days the road feels wide and sunlit. Other days, you stumble over the same stone you thought you'd already stepped past. That's not regression – that's reality. Healing isn't linear, and forgiveness isn't either – it's the gentle discipline of returning.

There are mornings when an old memory still stings, when I find myself replaying something I thought I'd released. In those moments, I try to meet myself with the same compassion I'd offer anyone else. I pause, breathe, and remember that I'm allowed to be both healed and healing at the same time.

Each return to forgiveness reveals something new. Maybe it's a pocket of grief I hadn't touched, or a layer of tenderness I'd been too scared to feel before. Staying with it – without judgment, without forcing it to look tidy – is where the healing happens, because the energy you once used to guard the wound becomes fuel for growth.

Forgiveness asks for patience. It asks you to keep showing up for your own freedom, even when it feels slow, even when it hurts. Because each time you come back, you unhook a little more from the past and stand a little taller in the present.

The Quiet After the Storm

When you've lived with pain long enough, peace can feel unfamiliar. The nervous system almost misses the drama, the rehearsed defenses, the constant readiness. But as forgiveness settles in, a new kind of stillness emerges. It's not the absence of feeling; it's the presence of space. You begin to notice the way light falls through the window, the way your breath reaches all the way down again. There's room for joy now – room for life.

Forgiveness doesn't rewrite what happened. It rewrites your relationship to it. You stop needing to win the argument in your head. You stop explaining your pain to people who can't understand it. You simply accept that the past shaped you, but it doesn't define you.

That's what it means to say, "It wasn't okay, but I am."

When I think about forgiveness now, I think about energy. Every time we forgive, we call our energy back home. We stop scattering ourselves across memories and what-ifs. We return to the truth of who we are – whole, imperfect, and still capable of love. That's the gift forgiveness gives you: the quiet after the storm, the breath after the release, the steady knowing that you are free.

"Grief doesn't ask for closure.

It asks to be felt."

Chapter 5: Grief and the Love That Lingers

Grief is not limited to the confines of funerals and black clothing. It also exists in the quiet ache after a friendship fades, the hollowness when a marriage ends, even in the confusion when your identity shifts and the person in the mirror feels unfamiliar. It's also the moment you realize a long-held expectation is not going to happen the way you planned. Grief is any place love or attachment has to reorganize itself around change.

And as with many things in life, with grief we often look for a finish line. We want to believe we can be "done" if we do it right. But grief doesn't work like that. It asks for presence, not performance. It asks for breath, not explanations. It asks to be felt. You can't think your way through it, because as I've said before, healing doesn't happen in the mind. It happens in the body.

So we begin where we are. With the thud in the chest, the fog in the head, the tightness in the throat, and the heaviness behind the eyes. Again, these are signs your nervous system is trying to protect you, which isn't failure;

it's design. When you can meet your body's signals with curiosity, rather than judgment, you will begin to move with grief instead of against it.

This isn't easy work, but it's what gets us through the long seasons of grief – sitting with the truth that love and loss live side by side, understanding that endings create space, and getting clear that feeling what hurts is how we remember what matters.

Pebbles, Two-By-Fours, And A Bracelet

Sometimes the "big" lessons arrive through very small doors. One weekend, my laptop refused to turn on. Ten minutes. Then twenty. In that gap, my mind sprinted: everything is lost, nothing is recoverable, how will I do the work I promised? When the screen finally lit up, I exhaled – and smiled. I had just been given a safe, tiny rehearsal for loss. A pebble, not a boulder.

I pay attention to pebbles now – an image I heard Oprah talk about – how when the universe wants our attention it starts with a pebble, then a two-by-four, then a boulder if we're not listening. I've learned to listen sooner because I know when I can notice the small griefs, I'm more prepared to cope when the larger ones come.

Years ago, a gold bracelet I'd worn since I was thirteen slipped off. I looked down, and it was simply...gone. It was "just" a thing, and also it wasn't. For a while I found myself bargaining – What if I had looked sooner? I mentally retraced routes, all the while feeling the pinch of absence. That little loss taught me something true: we carry grief in layers. The small ones echo the big ones; the big ones wake up the small ones.

These micro-griefs aren't frivolous. They are practice. Each one invites us to notice what we cling to, how quickly our bodies brace, how reflexively our minds catastrophize. Each one invites us to be gentle with ourselves.

Redefining Loss (So We Can Tell The Truth)

Loss is the simple fact of no longer being able to maintain someone or something. That spans a lot of life: the loss of a loved one or a pet, the loss of a job or a home, the loss of health, the loss of a marriage, the loss of a version of yourself you thought you had to be. There is also the loss of opportunity – the phone call you didn't return, the dream you postponed until later – and the loss of control, which touches almost everything.

Naming loss clearly is not negative thinking; it's honesty, and it helps your body settle. When we minimize, our nervous systems work harder to hold the contradiction. When we tell the truth – *this mattered to me, and I don't have it now* – our breath drops a little lower. We stop arguing with reality and start tending to ourselves within it.

Grief is the natural response to loss, one that shows up emotionally – shock, anger, disbelief, guilt, profound sadness – and physically: sleep disrupted, appetite altered, attention scattered, a chest that can't quite unclench. We carry it in the body.

If you've been waiting to "get over it," I want to offer a different frame: grief is less a hurdle to clear and more a landscape to learn. You don't have to love it. But you can learn its paths.

Moving In and Out of the Stages

I've walked with grief long enough to know it doesn't obey a calendar. Elizabeth Kubler Ross taught us about the five stages of grief – shock and denial, anger, bargaining, depression, acceptance – and those are real experiences. They are not, however, a straight staircase. You can touch anger in the morning and acceptance at lunch, circle back to bargaining by dinner, and wake into sadness the next day. It's not one and done.

Acceptance, when it arrives, isn't a goodbye to feeling. It's a softening around what's true. I've seen people live inside acceptance for years and still get surprised by a wave that knocks them sideways at a song, a scent, an anniversary. That doesn't mean you're back at the beginning. It means you're human.

When we demand linear progress from something that is cyclical by nature, we create unnecessary suffering. We start grading ourselves, demanding, *Am I normal? Am I doing this right?* But the only "right" thing is what is real for you right now. Your grief has a rhythm – whatever it is, however it comes, trust it.

And when the wave comes, meet it in your body before you try to make sense of it. Put a hand on your chest. Breathe. Feel into it, before you try to put it into words.

The Many Rooms Of Grief

Death is a profound loss, but grief is bigger than death alone. We grieve divorces and breakups, even when ending was truly necessary. We grieve transitions: the house that held a decade of memories, the daily routines that kept us steady, the role that gave us purpose. We grieve identity – the version of ourselves anchored to a relationship, a job, a parent, a child, a plan.

Sometimes you don't recognize your face for a while. That's part of it. The mirror asks, Who are you if you're not this person's partner, this company's employee, this family's caretaker, this dream's pursuer? Grief answers slowly. You might not love the answer right away. Stay with it though, because it is never too late to heal, grow, love, or reclaim your light.

Chronic illness and caregiving carry their own grief. There can be shock even when you've "prepared" for years. Anticipatory grief doesn't cancel the impact of the moment. It just means your heart has been stretching over time. Let that count.

If you've been the one keeping everyone else afloat, grief may insist you put yourself back on your own list. If you find yourself in that place, keep in mind that it isn't selfish of you – it's necessary to keep your own head above water.

Anger, Longing, Love and Permission

Grief is rarely tidy. Anger sits beside longing; love sits beside resentment; relief can sit beside sorrow. You may feel angry with the person who died – at their choices, their timing, even their silence as they moved towards their exit. You may feel angry with an ex even as you miss the family you built. You may feel relief that the suffering ended or guilt that relief is present at all.

Mixed emotions are not proof you're doing it wrong. They are proof you're doing it, period.

Permission helps, so give yourself permission to be mad, permission to laugh at something small, permission to feel joy without betraying what you lost. There is no referee throwing flags when it comes to grief. There is only your breath and your truth.

When it comes to anniversaries of loss – be gentle with yourself. Often, the weeks leading up to "the day" are harder than the day itself because of anticipation. Try making a plan that honors where you are in your process of grieving. Do you want company or solitude? A ritual, or just quiet reflection? Decide what works for you – and give yourself the right to change your mind when the morning comes.

And when a happy moment brings you back to sadness, that's not a failure of healing. That's love reminding you it still knows the way.

Community And The Courage To Tell Your Story

One of the most healing sentences we can utter when it comes to supporting someone through grief? "Tell me everything," because it's such a gift to let a grieving person speak about their loss. It makes the heaviness of what's inside them more bearable.

For years I facilitated survivor-after-suicide groups, and the first session was always the same: tell your story. More than stating the facts though, it meant speaking the unspeakable out loud in a room where no one looked away. It didn't fix the loss, but it helped to make it more bearable.

We need communities like that – ones that can hold us without trying to 'solve' grief for us. We need presence more than platitudes. Some days the most loving thing you can do for someone grieving is sit on the couch, pass the tissues, keep the kettle warm, and say very little. If you're the one grieving, ask for what would actually help.

I've also seen neighborhoods become families – meals delivered, logistics handled, passwords located, errands shared – so that the person grieving could grieve. Let people love you like that. It is not weakness to receive – it's how we remember we belong to each other.

And if you catch yourself saying, "I should be over this by now," borrow my voice: No. You're allowed to carry what you carry, and you're allowed to be comforted by your community.

How To Support (And What Not To Say)

A grieving person is living through something that cannot be fixed. Attempts to make it better too quickly are often premature and that can be unintentionally shaming. "At least..." sentences (at least he lived a long life, at least you can have another baby, at least you have your health) slam into tender hearts. Meet them with curiosity instead, *How is today? What feels hardest? Would it help to talk or to be quiet together?*

Expect their needs to change day by day. Some will want daily check-ins. Others will need space, so ask, don't assume. And remember the practical: offering to help with laundry, paperwork, childcare, rides, or food can be a lifeline, because grief drains our ability to function, making ordinary tasks feel like mountains. Let them know you're there to help with the climb.

If you're the griever, boundary is not rejection; it's honesty, so speak up and say, *"I don't have capacity for visitors this week." "Please text before calling." "I need one person to coordinate offers of help."* Clear lines protect your energy and help to be truly supportive.

And a gentle note about children: be simple, clear, and concrete. Avoid saying someone "went to sleep," because little nervous systems take language literally, and we do not want to pair bedtime with death. Say what happened in words they can hold, then sit beside them while feelings move through.

Practice: Meeting Grief In The Body

When the wave of grief rises, come back to the basics. Sit. Feel your feet on the floor and bring a hand to your heart. Notice whether your chest feels tight, hollow, full, buzzing, dull – whatever your body reports is information, rather than a problem. Just focus on noticing, and receiving one slow breath return to your body and meet yourself where you are.

Scan your throat. So much grief collects there – the ache before tears, the pressure of words unsaid. Soften that space with your attention. You don't have to force anything open. Your body knows what to do when you give it time.

Name what visits: whether it's sorrow, anger, love, disappointment, or gratitude, you don't need to feed the feelings or push them away. Let them crest and recede, and if you feel overwhelmed, pause. Take a drink of water, step outside into the fresh air and come back when you can.

Reflection is medicine – consider questions like: *How has loss shaped me? Where has it cracked me open to more compassion – for myself, for others? What do I want to remember about who and what I love, now?*

A Closing For The Road You're On

You don't have to rush to "move on." You're allowed to carry grief with you and still build a beautiful life. Know that there will be days you forget you're strong, where it feels like grief will overwhelm you. Just keep choosing the next honest breath, listening to your body, and trusting the love that lingers.

Grief isn't a problem to solve; it's a relationship to honor. Know that your healing won't be linear – allow yourself to feel all the way through it.

“Failure is a redirect. A necessary reroute. Not a dead end.”

Chapter 6: What If Failure Is the First Step

Grace Before Growth

Before we can even talk about failure, I always begin with grace. Because most of us start this conversation already braced – holding our breath, waiting for the judgment that so often follows the word *fail*. In my sessions, on the mic, even in my own mirror, I remind myself: *You're doing your best. You are enough right now.*

When we stop chasing perfection and settle into our breath, something softens. We begin to feel the difference between the voice that says *you should be doing more* and the quieter truth beneath it – the one that whispers, *you're okay right here.* That's the place healing begins. I've learned that you can't move through failure from your head; the mind only loops through the guilt and the what-ifs. Healing doesn't happen in the mind. It happens in the body – in the exhale that releases shame, in the inhale that brings you back to yourself.

So before I dive into the stories of what didn't work, I want you to take a breath with me. Let yourself exhale the perfectionism, the guilt, the 'shoulds.' Breathe in acceptance, breathe out shame. That's what I guided listeners through when I spoke about failure on my show – through breathing not as a performance, but as a practice. A way to remind your nervous system that you are safe even when things fall apart. You are not failing; you are feeling. And that is sacred work.

Redefining the F-Word

Why does failure get such a bad rap? It's not one of the worst F-words. In truth, it's one of our most faithful teachers. For so long, I believed failure meant I wasn't enough – that missing an expectation somehow made *me* the mistake. But failure, I've come to see, is simply a lack of alignment between what we hoped for and what happened. It's information. It shows us where our expectations were unrealistic, or where we were living by someone else's "should."

I've talked earlier about those first *Feel to Heal* episodes – how fear and perfectionism made me believe I had to sound polished and in control before I deserved to be heard. I still smile when I think about that version of me, because she was trying so hard to get it "right." By the time I revisited that memory later in my healing, I realized it wasn't really a story about podcasting at all; it was a story about visibility.

The deeper lesson wasn't how many times I had to stop and compose myself, or how my emotions took over, it was how willing I was to show up when fear told me not to. Every imperfection became evidence that authenticity connects more deeply than performance. That same truth has followed me into every area of life: in my work, in motherhood, in my friendships – in all my relationships. The moment you let go of performing, and stop worrying about where or not you might fail, you are able to be more present, and more authentic.

When we redefine failure, we reclaim our power from shame. Failing at something doesn't mean you *are* a failure. It means you tried. It means you stretched. It means you stepped outside the safety of what you already knew. Each stumble, each awkward beginning, becomes proof that you are alive and learning. You can't think your way through that kind of transformation – you have to feel it. That's how resilience is built, breath by breath.

Fear, Shame, and the Stories We Carry

Fear of failure lives in almost everyone I know. Studies show it ranks higher than the fear of public speaking or even spiders – but I see it every day in therapy rooms, boardrooms, and dinner tables. The fear of not getting it right, of being judged, of trying and falling short. We get caught in those old stories: *What if I fail again? What if it proves I'm not enough?*

When we've been shamed for making mistakes, failure starts to feel dangerous. Our bodies remember the tension, the disappointment, the look on someone's face when we didn't measure up. So we stop trying. We stay safe. We shrink. But that safety comes at a cost. When we're ruled by fear, we trade the aliveness of risk for the numbness of control.

That's why I say the only real failures are the ones that stop us from trying again. The rest are lessons, invitations to learn something new about ourselves. Truly, there are really only three ways to fail: when we quit, when we don't learn, or when we never try. Everything else is movement. Everything else is living.

When Failing Feels Personal

I used to take failure to mean I was broken. When I failed out of college after my sophomore year, I carried so much shame I could barely speak it aloud. I told myself stories about being lazy, about not belonging, about letting my parents down. What I didn't know then was that I had undiagnosed ADD. I was struggling under the weight of expectations – not because I wasn't capable, but because I hadn't yet learned how *I* needed to learn.

Eventually, I petitioned to go back, took summer courses, and did the work to rebuild, one credit, one breath, one self-forgiving thought at a time. That moment taught me something profound: I could start over. I could fail, and still choose to rise. Years later, when I earned my master's degree with honors, it wasn't the grades that mattered – it was the grace. It was knowing that my intelligence had never been reflected by a report card. Failure had redirected me toward the truth.

Sometimes failure is the only doorway big enough to walk you home to yourself. When you look back, you realize you didn't fail; you were being re-routed toward who you were always meant to become.

Parenting, Expectations, and Permission to Fall

Now, as a mom, I see how early we teach children to fear mistakes. We celebrate straight-A's but rarely celebrate the messy middle. All three of my kids have what's called a "three-five" profile in human design – which means the first 30 years of their lives are meant to be full of bumping into things, both literally and figuratively. It is about the experiences and the lessons. That insight gave me such peace. It reminded me that trial and error *is* the path.

So when one of my daughters decided college wasn't for her, I didn't panic. She had given it her best. She knew it wasn't her direction. And she's thriving in the real world, learning through experience, moving up with every job. Watching her claim her own definition of success affirmed what I already believed: failing isn't falling apart; it's finding your way.

As parents, mentors, friends – we have to stop rescuing people from the discomfort of trying. But we can love them through it without taking away the gift of learning. Because failure is never the end of the story. It's just one of the ways we learn to tell the truth about who we are.

The Ego and the Mind's Tricks

When failure stings, it's often our ego that's hurting, not our soul. The ego loves control. It wants to protect us from embarrassment, from vulnerability, from uncertainty. It will whisper, *Don't do that, you might fail again.* But the body – your deeper knowing – holds another truth. It remembers that you've survived every fall so far.

I tell my clients that the mind's job is to keep you safe and alive, so it will avoid risk even when your heart longs to grow. That's why healing from failure often means retraining the nervous system. You breathe, you move, and you remind yourself that trying again isn't fatal. The ego fears death in every risk, but the spirit knows that each ending is just another beginning.

When you can witness those old fear thoughts – *I can't, I'll mess up again, I'm not ready* – without obeying them, you start to build emotional muscle. That's what resilience really is: staying with yourself through the fall, instead of abandoning who you are.

Lessons From the "Bag of Failures"

In my twenties, I attended a workshop where the facilitator told us to come in the next day with our "bag of failures." I remember thinking, *Oh God, am I going to have to share these out loud?* I didn't even know what to bring – physical objects or just memories? The next morning, someone walked in with an actual bag filled with symbols of their mistakes. Seeing that shifted something in me. It made failure tangible – something you could hold, examine, learn from, and then put down.

I realized that failure only owns you when you hide it. Once you face it, it loses its power. That's why I often say to clients, "Let's take it out of the shadows." When you name it, breathe with it, and tell the truth about it, you reclaim your energy from shame. You begin to see that you were never defined by what went wrong – you were defined by how you kept showing up after.

That practice has stayed with me. When I feel that sting of embarrassment or regret, I picture dropping another object into that imaginary bag – and then, when I'm ready, setting it down again. That's how we turn pain into wisdom.

Failure as the Foundation

Regardless of how you feel about her politics, one of my favorite quotes is from J.K. Rowling: "Rock bottom became the solid foundation on which I rebuilt my life." I love that line because it captures what I've lived. I no longer think of hitting rock bottom as a horrible place to land. Instead, it's the ground that finally holds. I know what it feels like to hit that place – when you think you can't recover, and then somehow, grace lifts you.

Failure strips away what isn't true. It forces you to see what actually matters. When everything falls apart, you meet the unshakable part of yourself that doesn't. That's where real power begins – not in perfection, but in presence.

When we can meet our failures with compassion instead of condemnation, we begin to trust ourselves again. We remember that falling isn't evidence of weakness; it's proof of participation. You're in the game. You're growing. You're becoming.

The Courage to Keep Going

I think about all the people we admire who could have stopped after their first setback – Oprah being fired from her news job, Michael Jordan being cut from his high-school team, J.K. Rowling being rejected again and again and again. They kept going, not because they didn't fail, but because they refused to *stop*. That's the difference between failure and success – it's not as much about talent as it is about willingness.

Every time you fall and rise again, your nervous system learns safety in the unknown. You teach your body that it can survive disappointment, that it can tolerate risk, that it can feel the sting and still keep its heart open. That's emotional resilience – and it's built one imperfect attempt at a time.

So if you've failed recently, take a breath. You're in sacred territory. You're being refined, not rejected. Every misstep is an invitation back to truth, to trust, to self-compassion. Failure isn't your enemy. It's your initiation.

Fail Forward With Grace

Failure is not the opposite of success; it's the teacher that makes success possible. Every time you fall, you're given a choice – to close off or to open, to hide or to heal. If you can stay present long enough to feel what it brings up – the shame, the grief, the disappointment – it will transform into wisdom.

Let the breath lead you there. Breathe in grace, breathe out judgment. Remember: failure isn't who you are, it's just a moment asking for your attention. When you meet it with compassion, it becomes a doorway to deeper self-trust.

You are doing your best. You are already enough. And sometimes, the first step on the path to healing is simply this: allowing yourself to fall, to fail, and then to begin again.

"Anger is a truth-teller. I just had to get quiet enough to hear it."

Chapter 7: Anger as a Compass, Not a Crime

We all grow up with messages about what's acceptable to feel. Some of us are told not to cry, not to raise our voice, not to rock the boat. I was one of those people who learned to stay small and stay pleasant. I thought being "nice" was the same as being good. The problem is, when you're always trying to be nice, you end up disconnecting from what's real. You silence yourself before anyone else ever has to.

Over time, those unspoken rules start to shape the way we see ourselves, and we take on labels that don't really belong to us – *too emotional, too much, too sensitive* – because somewhere along the way, someone said those words and we believed them. I began to notice how easily those labels slipped into my own self-talk, how they became a quiet script I lived by. And the moment I started paying attention to the words I used to describe myself, everything started to shift. Awareness was the first step. When I finally got honest, I could see that "nice" had become a label that kept me quiet, and it was time to put it down.

For a long time, I also believed that staying calm meant I was handling things well. I would feel anger rising in my body and tell myself, *No, that's not who you are.* But emotions don't disappear just because you ignore them. They go somewhere. They sit in your body, waiting to be felt.

At that point I started to see anger less as an enemy, and more as a messenger. It was my body's way of saying, "Something's not right here." And once I stopped trying to push it away, I could finally listen. That's what I mean when I say anger is a truth-teller. It shows you what matters. It brings you back to yourself.

Where Does It Go When We Don't Let It Out?

In the work I do, I talk a lot about the body and the nervous system, because healing doesn't happen in the mind, it happens in the body. When we don't allow ourselves to feel what we feel, it doesn't vanish; it shows up physically. The body keeps it until we move it through.

When you experience a crisis, you don't just experience it your mind – your body experiences it as well. That's what anger does. It floods your system, quickens your breath, tightens your muscles. And when you keep trying to pretend you're fine, that energy has nowhere to go. You end up living with the side effects – tension, headaches, fatigue – without realizing it's just an emotion that never had a chance to finish its cycle.

I've seen this over and over. Someone says, "I don't know why I'm anxious all the time," but then as soon as they start to breathe and name what's really there, their anxiety softens. I often tell people that it helps to go into breathwork to begin lessening your stress response. So when you find yourself triggered and experiencing an intense emotion like anger, receive a breath, always go back to the breath, and then ride the emotional wave. Eventually, it's going to end."

That's the practice. Not pushing it away or judging it, but letting yourself feel what you feel. When you ride the wave instead of fighting it, you discover that anger isn't endless. It moves through and leaves behind something steadier – clarity, truth, and a little more space to breathe.

The Harm Of Bypassing Anger In The Name Of Spirituality

For a long time, I thought I was doing the right thing by staying positive. I believed that being spiritual meant forgiving quickly, focusing on love, and moving on. But what I was really doing was bypassing what I felt. I was putting light on top of darkness and calling it grace.

Bypassing anger doesn't make it go away. It just buries it deeper. And when you bury something alive, it will find another way to be seen – through your body, your relationships, or your exhaustion. True spirituality isn't about denying pain; it's about being able to hold it without losing yourself in it.

There's nothing unspiritual about anger. You can be deeply loving and still be mad. You can forgive and still have boundaries. You can want peace and still tell the truth. That's what wholeness looks like. It's allowing yourself to feel the full range of emotion – grief, fear, sadness, joy, and yes, anger – and knowing that none of it makes you less evolved.

I used to think if I stayed in love and light, I could avoid the hard parts. But the truth is, love and light are only real when they're grounded in truth. Feeling anger doesn't take you away from your spirit; it brings you closer to it. It's your body's way of saying, "You matter. Pay attention."

The Body Keeps The Score

When you don't give your anger an outlet, it will keep coming back to you in physical form -- tightness in your chest, tension in your shoulders, knots in your stomach, maybe even a headache that lingers for days. Your body will hold on to what your mind refuses to face.

I've been through this many times myself – anger, irritability, mood swings, that feeling of being on edge – all showing up for apparently no reason. And let's be clear, these are not character flaws; they're signs that your nervous system is still carrying old pain. But when you understand that what's happening is your body trying to protect you, it starts to shift. Instead of judging yourself, you can start to listen.

Sometimes healing looks like shaking. Sometimes it looks like crying. Sometimes it's a long walk, a deep sigh, or finally saying the words you've swallowed for years. That's your body doing what it knows how to do – moving energy that was never meant to stay stuck.

Feeling your anger doesn't mean losing control. It's what allows control to return. When you let your body finish the cycle, you clear space for something softer to emerge – relief, calm, and the quiet knowing that you've told yourself the truth. That's what healing feels like: the body remembering that it's safe again.

The Courage To Speak Your Truth

Finding the courage to give anger a voice was one of the most powerful shifts in my own healing. For years I believed that speaking up would make things worse – that if I stayed quiet and agreeable, the conflict would pass. But silence doesn't heal anything. It just teaches you to disappear in plain sight.

Real courage isn't about shouting or convincing anyone else to see things your way. It's about being honest with yourself first, so you can stop explaining away what hurts and start telling the truth about it. It can sound as simple as, *That doesn't work for me,* or *I need something different.* Small sentences like these can be the beginning of freedom.

I've seen this happen many times with clients, where someone who has spent years questioning their own reality finally begins to trust themselves again. They start writing things down – what was said, what was felt – and suddenly the confusion clears. They can see what was manipulation, what was gaslighting, and what was actual truth. The next time they're told they're "too sensitive," they can take a breath and remember: *I hear you, and I don't have to agree.* That's not defiance; that's self-respect.

The first time I spoke from that place of clarity, my body shook. Every muscle expected backlash. But when I stayed present with my breath, the fear gave way to calm. I realized I didn't need to raise my voice to be heard; I only needed to stand in my own truth. That's the power of allowing ourselves to experience our anger – it helps to reveal our own steady, clear truth.

When Anger Turns To Clarity

Anger often shows up first, but it's rarely the whole story. If you stay with it long enough, you start to feel what's underneath, the grief, the hurt, the disappointment, the longing to be understood. Anger is the signal; clarity – and truth – is what comes after you listen.

When you stop judging yourself for being angry, you can meet that part of you with compassion instead of shame. You begin to understand that the anger was never against anyone, it was for you. It was protecting the part that still wanted to be seen, heard, and safe.

I've learned that compassion is the antidote to anger that hardens. It's not about excusing harm or pretending everything is fine. It's about remembering that most people act from their own pain, and seeing that clearly allows you to release what isn't yours to carry. Compassion softens the edges so you can hold boundaries without bitterness.

When anger turns into clarity, it gives you direction instead of destruction. You know what matters. You know what needs to change. You can act, speak, or let go from a grounded place. That's when anger stops being chaos and becomes a compass.

Practicing Safe Expression

Learning to move anger safely through the body has been one of the most transformative parts of healing – for me and for so many others. Anger itself isn't the problem; it's what we do with it that matters. Most of us were never taught how to express it in a way that feels safe. We either explode or implode. We lash out, or we shut down. We take it out on the wrong person, or we turn it in on ourselves.

What I've come to understand is that anger is energy, and it needs somewhere to go. If you can pause in the moment and remember to breathe, you interrupt the pattern. You move from reaction to response. When I feel that familiar surge in my chest, I bring my attention back to my body: *What's happening inside me right now? Where am I holding this?* I breathe into it. I let the wave move through instead of trying to stop it.

This is what I mean when I say "ride the emotional wave." It will crest, it will break, and it will pass. The breath is your anchor. It reminds your nervous system that you're safe enough to feel. You don't have to fix the feeling or push it away – you just have to stay with it until it moves.

If you've kept yourself from expressing your anger for a long time, keep in mind that the intensity of what you feel may not belong to the present moment. And while it can be tempting to unload on whoever's closest, be mindful of the fact that you may be subjecting someone to feelings that stem from a distant, long ago event.

Awareness will help you bring that energy back home to its source, to where you can meet it with compassion rather than projection. That's how anger becomes clean, rather than being suppressed or weaponized. Awareness shifts it to where it becomes just energy being moved through honesty, breath, and presence.

Reclaiming The Power Beneath The Fire

There's a scene in the old movie *Network* that I've always loved, the one where people throw their televisions out their windows because they're mad and they're 'not going to take it anymore!' It's dramatic and raw and a little absurd, but there's something so human about it. That moment of collective exhale, of finally saying "enough," is exactly what reclaiming your power feels like.

For so long, I mistook peace for silence. I thought being agreeable made me loving, that saying "yes" kept me safe. But real peace doesn't come from pretending. It comes from authenticity. When you stop apologizing for what you feel, you stop abandoning yourself. You stop living for permission.

Reclaiming your anger isn't about rebellion; it's about remembering that you have a choice, and that leads to a deep inner shift when you realize, *I can't keep doing this the same way anymore*. Anger becomes the voice of truth rising from within, guiding you back to your boundaries, your voice, your center.

I've watched people reach this turning point countless times. A client who finally says, "No, I won't do that anymore." A parent who stops taking the blame for everyone else's feelings. A woman who realizes that loving herself sometimes means disappointing others. That's the moment the fire becomes freedom.

You already hold the power to release old pain, rewrite limiting stories, and step into a life of healing, freedom, and authentic self-expression. Anger is just one of the ways that power introduces itself. When you let yourself feel it fully, you come home to your own strength.

Let Anger Lead You Home

Anger is not something to fix or overcome. It's a guide that points to where you've been silencing yourself, where your boundaries need attention, and where your truth has been waiting to be spoken. It can feel uncomfortable at first – the rush of heat, the tightness in your chest, the racing thoughts. But if you can stay with it, breathe into it, and trust that it's leading somewhere meaningful, the discomfort softens into understanding. You begin to see that your anger was never against you; it was for you. It was your body saying, "Come back. There's something here you've been ignoring."

Every emotion we have carries a message. Anger's message is often about truth and boundaries. It says, *Pay attention. You matter.* When you give yourself permission to listen, you start to live in deeper integrity with who you are. You stop betraying yourself for comfort or approval. You begin to act from love instead of fear.

The next time you feel anger rise, pause. Notice where it is in your body. Take a slow breath and ask, *What are you trying to tell me?* You don't have to analyze it or explain it, just listen. When you honor anger as the teacher it is, it can lead you somewhere softer: clarity, safety, and self-respect.

Closing Reflection

Healing isn't about avoiding what's hard; it's about learning to stay with yourself through it. Anger, like every emotion, wants to move. When you let it move through your body instead of turning it inward, it loses its charge and leaves behind wisdom.

You are not broken for feeling angry. You are human. Your nervous system is doing its best to protect you until it knows it's safe. When you meet that fire with compassion, you reclaim your power, not by controlling emotion, but by listening to it. Let anger remind you that your truth matters. Let it clear away what no longer fits. Let it show you what needs tending. When you can feel anger without fear, that's when you'll be on your way to true freedom.

"I didn't love myself because I should. I learned to love myself because I listened."

Chapter 8: Loving Yourself Without the Hashtag

For a long time, I confused love with effort. I believed that if I kept working on myself, if I kept fixing and doing, eventually I would arrive at a version of me who was worthy of love. What I didn't realize was that all that doing kept me from hearing what my body and heart were already trying to tell me. The work wasn't in striving – it was in softening. When I finally stopped performing, even for myself, something began to shift. I started to notice my breath, the stillness underneath the noise, the quiet voice that said, *you are already enough.*

Self-love, I've come to understand, begins with allowing. When I allow myself to slow down, I can feel that I am held by something larger – a light that has been here all along. I sometimes imagine it as a wash of color – greens, blues, yellows, white – moving through me, cleansing the parts of me that have worked too hard to prove anything. I breathe into that, and with every breath I remind myself that I don't have to be more or do more to be worthy of my own love.

This kind of love doesn't come with conditions. It's not a reward for good behavior or a prize for perfection. It's grace. It's tenderness. It's the soft understanding that I am lovable in my mistakes, my chaos, and my calm. The more I listen, the more I can feel that love living inside me. Healing doesn't happen in my mind – it happens in my body, when I let go of control and return to my own breath.

Loving myself isn't about standing taller or speaking louder; it's about grounding deeper into who I already am. It's letting love be something I feel rather than something I chase. Every time I remember that, I can meet myself right where I am – human, flawed, whole, and enough.

When Love Feels Out of Reach

Even when my life looked full – the career, the family, the relationships – there were days when love felt like something outside of me. I could give endlessly to others, yet I struggled to offer myself the same care. It's so easy to lose yourself in the roles you play – partner, parent, friend, therapist – and forget that you are a person underneath it all. I used to think that was what love looked like: showing up for everyone else first. But that kind of giving left me depleted. It kept me stuck in patterns of caretaking that felt familiar but never fulfilling.

I now see how deeply those patterns run. As women – and really, as humans – we've been conditioned to believe that love is measured by how much we give, how much we sacrifice. We learn early on to be the peacemakers and the fixers, to smooth things over before anyone even asks. But that kind of devotion can turn into disappearance. When all your energy goes to keeping others comfortable, there's little left for the parts of you that need comfort too.

It took me years to learn that self-love isn't selfish – it's essential. Love that depends on someone else's approval will always keep you waiting. Real love begins when you stop waiting to be chosen and choose yourself. For me, that has meant finding the balance between giving and receiving, between showing up for others and honoring what I need to stay grounded. It's a daily recalibration, an ongoing awareness of when my giving comes from fullness and when it's coming from fear.

I still catch myself, sometimes, slipping into old patterns. The voice that says *take care of them first* is still there, but I meet it now with compassion instead of guilt. I remind myself that loving others and loving myself aren't opposites – they're connected. When I'm anchored in my own worth, what I give becomes honest and alive. That's what real love feels like: not a performance, but a presence.

When Giving Turns Into Burnout

There was a time when I thought love meant saying yes to everyone else. I was the one who filled in, fixed, managed, soothed. I believed that the more I did, the more loving I was – until I found myself exhausted and resentful. I had mistaken depletion for devotion. I didn't realize that all my helping had quietly turned into self-abandonment.

What I see so clearly now is that codependency can feel like love when it's really survival. It's what happens when we forget that we have a self to return to. Somewhere along the line, we were told that good people don't need as much, that it's noble to put everyone else first. But that story keeps you small. It keeps you waiting for someone else to give you permission to rest.

I've had to learn that caring for others doesn't mean disappearing inside their needs. There's a difference between compassion and caretaking. Compassion says, *I'm here with you.* Caretaking says, *I'll lose myself to save you.* Only one of those leads to connection. The other leads to burnout.

These days I ask myself, *Am I giving from fullness or from fear?* When I give from fullness, there's ease – a steady rhythm that feels honest and alive. When I give from fear, it feels like tightening, like my breath is shorter. That's my cue to pause, to come back to my own center. Love that drains you isn't love at all; it's a call to remember where you end and someone else begins.

From Effort to Presence

For most of my life I thought growth meant effort – more reading, more fixing, more figuring it out. I kept trying to think my way into peace. But the mind can only take you so far. Healing happens in the body. It happens when you breathe and allow what's here instead of trying to control it.

When I sit in stillness, even for a moment, I can feel what's underneath all that striving. Sometimes it's fear, sometimes it's tenderness, sometimes it's just quiet. That's the doorway. The moment I stop running from it, I can feel my whole nervous system begin to settle. There's a softening that comes with allowing – a gentle exhale that says, *I don't have to fight this.*

Presence isn't about perfection. It's not about holding it together or doing it right. It's about noticing what's happening inside and letting it be. When I remember to breathe – truly breathe – I can feel the awareness that lives beneath every emotion, the steady place that never leaves. In that awareness, I find compassion for myself and for others.

What I love most about this practice is that it keeps me connected. The more present I am, the more I want to reach out, to share that same compassionate awareness with others. It's a circle – presence leads to love, and love deepens presence. That's how healing unfolds: one breath, one honest moment at a time.

Rebuilding Self-Trust

Rebuilding trust with myself has been one of the deepest parts of my healing. For years, I looked outside of me for validation – for someone to tell me I was doing it right, that I was enough, that I was lovable. I see now that waiting for that approval kept me disconnected from my own truth. It's not about waiting for anyone else to choose me. It's about choosing myself, again and again, no matter what is happening around me.

There's a line I come back to often: you can't pour from an empty cup. I used to laugh at that, but now I understand it in my bones. You have to fill your own cup first – and that's not selfish, it's sacred. It's putting on your own love mask before you try to love anyone else. It's knowing that your worth isn't measured by what you do for others; it's measured by the honesty with which you meet yourself.

For me, self-trust grows in the small, quiet choices – saying no when something doesn't feel right, speaking up even when my voice shakes, giving myself permission to rest without guilt. Each time I honor what's real for me, I remind my body that it can depend on me. That's how safety rebuilds – not through control, but through consistency.

Trust isn't built in grand gestures; it's built in presence. It's when I stop forcing myself to be better and start listening to what's true. I don't always get it right. But I no longer abandon myself when I get it wrong. I breathe, I feel, I stay. That's how I know the relationship I've been rebuilding – the one with me – is finally strong.

The Quiet Freedom of Choosing Yourself

What surprised me most about this journey is how peaceful it feels to simply be with myself. I used to think love would feel like fireworks – something big and loud. But real love, the kind that lasts, is quiet. It's steady. It doesn't need to be proven or performed. It's the gentle knowing that I am safe in my own company.

When I finally stopped trying to earn love, I started to experience freedom. I didn't have to chase anyone's approval or wait for permission to rest. I didn't have to perfect myself to be worthy. I could love myself, as I am, even while I'm still learning, still growing, still human. I could be a work in progress and still be enough.

This is the freedom that comes from choosing yourself – from recognizing that you are already whole. Every time I listen instead of perform, every time I slow down and breathe instead of pushing through, I feel that freedom deepening. It's a soft place to land inside myself.

It's not one and done. There are days I forget. There are moments when old habits whisper, *do more, be better*. But now I know those voices are just fear. They don't need to be silenced; they need to be met with love. I remind myself:

you are an eternal being of love and light. That's the truth beneath all the noise. And from that truth, I get to live – open, grounded, and free.

From Presence to Connection

The more you practice presence, the more connected you become – not only to yourself, but to everyone around you. When you're grounded in your own breath, you can meet people from a place of wholeness instead of need. You can listen without losing yourself in their stories. You can care deeply without carrying what isn't yours to hold.

What's beautiful about presence is that it doesn't ask you to be perfect – it just asks you to be here. When fear rises, notice it. Let it be welcome. Fear is only a feeling, a wave moving through your body. When you stop resisting it, it begins to soften, and what was once a barrier becomes a guide.

Fear is not the enemy; it's information. When you greet it with compassion instead of judgment, it reveals what you need – to rest, to speak, to release, to reach out. Every emotion carries its own message, and the more you listen, the more clearly you'll understand what your inner world is asking for.

Connection starts from within. When you can sit with your own discomfort, you create space for others to do the same. When you offer yourself grace, that grace naturally extends outward. Love expands when it's allowed to move freely – not forced, not performed, just honest and alive. That's the connection presence makes possible.

Listening, Again and Again

Love isn't a destination you reach; it's a rhythm you return to. Every time you pause long enough to listen, you'll find it waiting. It lives in the breath that steadies you, in the stillness that holds you, in the quiet truth that you are already enough.

Healing doesn't require you to become someone new. It asks you to remember who you've always been – a being of love and light. Even when you forget, even when you fall back into old patterns, love doesn't disappear. It waits for you to notice it again. So keep listening. Listen when you're tired, when you're angry, when you're uncertain. Listen when you don't have the answers. Listening is how love speaks – softly, through the body, through the breath, through presence.

You don't need to earn love. You need only to notice it. Every time you listen, you return to the truth that's been here all along: you are love.

"Sometimes pain means you're moving in the right direction – towards the person you're becoming."

Chapter 9: Birthing the New You (Even If It's Messy)

There's a moment in every transformation that feels like pressure – that sense of something inside you straining to become more than it was before. I've felt it again and again, that mixture of excitement and nausea, the pulse of something new trying to make its way into being. And just like with birth, there comes a time when you can't think your way through it. You have to feel your way through.

When I birthed my children, I learned that my body knew exactly what to do once I stopped trying to control it. I had to take my head out of the process and trust the wisdom that already lived inside me. The same thing happens when we birth a new version of ourselves. We tighten up, we resist, we brace against the pain – but the real growth begins when we exhale and let life move through us.

Sometimes we get stuck in the birth canal of our own becoming. I've been there – scared, overthinking, holding on to the familiar even when I knew something bigger was calling. It's human to be afraid. But pain isn't proof you're doing something wrong; it's often the sign that you're doing something brave. The discomfort you feel when everything is shifting is the contraction that brings you closer to truth.

So if you're feeling that squeeze right now – if life feels tight, uncertain, or messy – don't assume you're failing. You're in labor with your own becoming. You can breathe through it. You can let it unfold. The pressure that feels unbearable today might just be the force that delivers you to yourself.

The Stability in Change

It took me a long time to realize there is stability in change. We think of stability as sameness, but real stability is the knowing that change will come – always. You can count on it, and there's a strange kind of peace in that. When you stop fighting the inevitable, the fear loosens its grip.

Change is constant: day turns to night, seasons circle back, our cells renew without our permission. The problem isn't that things change; it's that we expect them not to. We brace against the shift instead of flowing with it. And when we fight change, we suffer. When we let it work through us, we grow.

I used to try to control every detail of my life, believing that if I planned carefully enough, I could avoid the chaos. But change has its own rhythm – it doesn't wait for your consent. The truth is, you have one hundred percent control over no control. Once you accept that, you can stop fighting the current and start floating with it.

There's freedom in remembering that life is happening *for* you, not *to* you. Every ending carries the seed of a beginning. So take a breath, and trust that the flow knows where it's going. You don't have to push against it anymore. You're allowed to be carried.

The Mess and the Meaning

Transformation rarely looks graceful. We imagine it should – a tidy rise into light, all serenity and insight – but the truth is, becoming who you're meant to be is messy. It's the kind of mess that comes when you're half in the old world and half in the new. I've lived through that space so many times – restless, scared, exhilarated – and every time I realize the same thing: the mess isn't a mistake. It's proof that something real is happening.

There have been moments where I thought I was falling apart, only to discover later that I was finally coming together. I was releasing the version of me who was trying too hard, holding too tight, and carrying too much. I used to think I had to get it "right" – that healing meant composure, stillness, a perfect plan. But healing isn't a performance – it's a process. It's crying in the car. It's forgetting your own advice. It's saying yes to something new while your whole nervous system is screaming no.

I know now that the fear, the nausea, even the self-doubt are all part of the birthing pains of change. You can't have transformation without contraction. You can't become new without shedding what no longer fits. That pressure you feel isn't punishment; it's movement. It's the universe saying, *something else is ready to be born.*

So when it all feels chaotic – when the petals of your life are falling in every direction – pause and look closer. You are still the same rose at the center of it all, blooming through the mess. There is meaning hidden in the soil of every moment. You just have to stop judging the dirt long enough to see what's growing there.

Surrendering to What Is

At some point in every journey, control stops working. The plans fall apart, the timing goes sideways, and your only choice is to surrender – not in defeat, but in trust. That's when you learn that surrender isn't giving up; it's giving over. It's softening into what's real instead of fighting to keep things as they were.

For me, surrender looked like finally exhaling after years of holding my breath. It meant letting go of the stories about how things "should" be and meeting myself exactly where I was. It wasn't comfortable. My mind resisted, my body tensed, and my heart tried to bargain. But life kept reminding me: you're safe enough to let go. You don't have to fight your own becoming.

I once imagined surrender as a fall – a loss of control, a descent into uncertainty. But now I see it as a gentle lowering back into truth, where the soil of your life holds you steady while something new takes root. The more I surrendered, the more I noticed the quiet strength inside me that had been there all along. That is where real transformation happens: not in the resistance, but in the release that occurs when you stop trying to outrun discomfort and start listening to it. That's when you start to realize your nervous system isn't the enemy; it's a guide. It's trying to protect you until you can remind it you're safe. And when you do, your whole being exhales. You soften into the truth that becoming is not about control – it's about trust.

So if you find yourself in that space where nothing feels certain, take one deep breath and let yourself be where you are. You don't have to fix it or rush it. You're already in motion. The process is happening for you. And even if you can't see it yet, something beautiful is already taking shape beneath the surface.

Learning from the Pain

Pain has a way of getting our attention. It interrupts, demands, and refuses to be ignored – and yet, when we stop running from it, it becomes one of our greatest teachers. I've learned that the moments I've wanted to escape the most were the moments that ended up expanding me the most. It's not that I've ever liked pain, I've stopped believing it means something has gone wrong. Sometimes it means I'm finally moving toward what's right.

Birthing something new – an idea, a boundary, a version of yourself – is going to hurt. There's no way around that. But there's a difference between pain that signals injury and pain that signals growth. The pain of growth comes with a pulse, an aliveness. It feels like pressure in the body, a stretching of the spirit. It's what happens when the seed cracks open, when the old shell can no longer contain what's growing inside. That cracking isn't failure – it's the necessary breaking that allows new life to take form.

There were times when I resisted it – when I begged the universe to make things easier, to make it stop. But the truth is, if life were always easy, we'd never grow roots deep enough to hold us steady. The moments that felt unbearable are the same ones that taught me strength, patience, and surrender. It's like I said once – if birthing a human without pain were effortless, we might do it more often, but we'd lose the reverence that comes with knowing what it costs.

So when you find yourself in pain, don't rush to escape it. Breathe into it. Ask the pain what it's here to teach you. Let it move through you the way contractions move through the body – intense, yes, but purposeful. There is wisdom inside every ache. It's showing you where the old pattern is ending and where the new self is ready to emerge.

The Ground Beneath You

When I guide people through change, I often ask them to imagine their own soil. Because no matter what you're growing, you need ground to stand on. Your soil is everything you've lived – the experiences, lessons, heartbreaks, and tiny moments of grace that make you who you are. You don't have to discard the past to grow something new; you just have to tend to it differently.

In one of my meditations, I invite people to picture a tender young shoot breaking through the earth. Its soil is rich with all that's come before – the joy, the pain, the lessons, the mistakes. That soil isn't "baggage." It's nourishment. Every experience feeds the next version of you. You get to choose what enriches your ground and what no longer belongs there. You can't control the weather, but you can care for the soil.

That's what stability really means. It's not about avoiding the storm; it's about knowing where to plant your roots when the storm comes. You build steadiness by being present, by feeling your feet on the ground, by remembering that you are safe even when everything around you is shifting. You don't have to have it all figured out. You just have to stay connected to yourself, to your breath, and to the knowing that you can grow through this too.

So take a moment to ask yourself: what's in your soil right now? What's nourishing you, and what's depleting you? You already have the wisdom to tell the difference. The ground beneath you isn't just holding you – it's teaching you how to grow. And if you listen closely, you'll hear it whispering the same truth it's whispered to me: *You are the shoot. You are the soil. You are still growing.*

Letting Change Work Through You

Change has a rhythm all its own. It doesn't ask for permission. It doesn't check your calendar or wait until you're ready. It moves through your life like water – sometimes gently, sometimes as a wave that catches you off guard. And the more you resist it, the more it pounds against you. The moment you stop fighting, though, it begins to carry you instead.

Letting change work through you doesn't mean you stop feeling afraid. It means you allow the fear to exist without letting it run the show. You breathe with it, not against it. You stop forcing clarity and start trusting the unfolding. You let yourself be surprised by what emerges once you stop trying to steer.

And in that space – between the letting go and the becoming – you find grace. You find that change isn't the enemy you thought it was; it's a companion, one that's been walking beside you all along. Every new beginning is just change, doing what it came to do: transform you from the inside out.

Honoring What Got You Here

Every version of you that has existed along the way deserves gratitude, not judgment. It's easy to look back and wish you'd known then what you know now, to cringe at the choices you made or the fears that held you back. But the truth is, those versions of you carried you through the storm. They got you here. They did the best they could with the tools they had.

When I reflect on my own life, I see the scaffolding of every experience – each stage building on the one before it. The mistakes, the waiting, the confusion – they were all part of the architecture of growth. You can't skip steps. You can't leap to wisdom without living through the mess that teaches it. Every chapter, even the painful ones, becomes part of your foundation.

That's what it means to honor what got you here. You stop seeing your past self as a problem to fix and start seeing her as a companion. You thank her for being brave enough to keep going, even when she didn't know how. You recognize that every detour was an education, and every delay was an invitation to deepen.

So pause for a moment and take stock of your own becoming. Notice the patience it took to get here, the small acts of courage you didn't even realize were courage at the time. Maybe you outgrew something that once defined you. Maybe you spoke a truth that scared you. Maybe you learned to rest when you used to run. Whatever it is, honor it.

You are the sum of all your experiences. Each one has enriched the soil you're growing from. Each one has taught you to trust yourself a little more. When you can see that clearly, the shame falls away. You begin to understand that you were never broken – you were always becoming.

A Final Reflection: You Are Becoming

There comes a moment in every birthing process when you realize you've been holding your breath – waiting for the moment it all makes sense, for the pain to stop, for the clarity to arrive. Becoming isn't a single moment of arrival. It's a rhythm, a lifelong expansion. You breathe, you contract, you expand again. And each cycle brings you closer to the truth of who you are.

You don't have to have it all figured out. You don't need to rush the process or make it look beautiful. The soil gets messy, the contractions come when you least expect them, and sometimes you forget how strong you really are. That's okay. You're human. You're learning how to stay open in the middle of transformation, and that's sacred work.

So be gentle with yourself as you grow. Be patient with the parts of you that still ache, still doubt, still want to cling to what was. Every part of you belongs. Every experience – even the painful ones – has been shaping you for this moment. You are not behind. You are not late. You are exactly where you need to be on your own path of becoming.

Remember this: growth doesn't happen in the mind. It happens in the body. It happens in the breath, in the tears, in the quiet moments when you finally let yourself rest. Healing isn't about getting back to who you were; it's about becoming who you are. It's not one and done. It's not linear. It's the ongoing practice of trusting yourself, again and again, even when it's hard.

So take one more deep breath. Feel your feet on the ground. Know that everything that has happened has been preparing you for this – the breaking, the blooming, and the becoming.

"You can't think your way to healing. You have to feel your way through."

Chapter 10:
The Only Way Out Is Through

No matter how long we've spent running from our emotions or pretending we're fine, the moment we choose to stop and feel what's real – that's when healing begins. We spend so much time avoiding feelings, thinking that if we keep busy, if we stay distracted, the discomfort will somehow pass. And doing nothing is still doing something. When we numb out or shut down, we're still feeding the cycle of avoidance. So why not choose to feel instead?

Even when the feelings are awful, even when they suck, they still deserve space to move through us. That's what allows them to shift. When I finally stopped judging my emotions and started letting them exist – no editing, no resistance – I realized how much of my pain came from trying to control them. Feeling what's real doesn't mean drowning in sadness or staying stuck in anger. It means allowing every emotion to have its moment and trusting that it will pass once it's been acknowledged. It's never too late to do that – to allow your feelings to move through you.

Stress and fear are often what keep us from opening that door. They whisper that we'll be overwhelmed, that we can't handle what's waiting inside. But stress and fear are just thoughts that live in the mind, not truths that live in the body. They hold us back from doing what we want, what we need, what our heart is asking for. We get stuck in our heads, analyzing every feeling instead of letting it be felt. Healing begins when we stop trying to think our way through and start letting ourselves feel our way through.

The Stories That Keep Us Stuck

So much of our suffering comes from the stories we tell ourselves – stories about time, control, and comparison. Time can feel like our biggest enemy, the ticking clock reminding us of everything we haven't done. But time isn't against us; it's just moving forward naturally, as it always has and always will. It's our thoughts about time that create pressure. We measure and compare, always asking if we're behind, if it's too late, if someone else is further ahead. But what if you stopped comparing altogether? What if you accepted that you are exactly where you're meant to be?

You have no control over the past or the future. You can't change what's already happened, and worrying about what's next only pulls yesterday's pain into tomorrow. The only moment that truly belongs to you is now – this breath, this heartbeat, this feeling. That's where healing lives. Stillness isn't about stopping time; it's about dropping out of the noise and remembering that everything you need is already here.

The truth is, we've all been conditioned to look outward for validation – to care deeply about what others think of us, to worry about how we're perceived. But that's not your work. It's not your job to manage anyone else's opinions or expectations. The only thing you have control over is how you show up: your thoughts, your boundaries, your actions, your attention. When you stop trying to fix what's outside of you and start tending to what's within, everything changes; after all, healing isn't about controlling life, it's about surrendering to it.

Time, Change, and Stillness

Time never stops for any of us, despite our efforts to measure it, bend it, and control it. What I've learned is that while I have no control over time passing, I do have control over how I choose to pass the time. I get to choose whether I will resist, or allow – whether I will stop fighting and be still.

When you let yourself be still, you discover that stillness has no opinion. It doesn't judge, compare, or quantify. It's the space where time moves around you instead of through you. In that space, you can finally hear your own truth. You can feel without commentary, without trying to fix or analyze. That's what being present really means – sitting with what's here, even when it's uncomfortable, and trusting that you can handle it.

Time can only hurt us when we use it as a weapon against ourselves. When we look back and call it wasted, or look ahead and call it running out, we separate ourselves from the present. But in the stillness, time simply is. It becomes an ally, not an enemy. It's never too late to be still, never too late to pause, breathe, and allow yourself to exist without rushing toward the next thing.

Saying Yes to What Scares You

It's also never too late to start something new. It's never too late to be scared and say yes anyway. I've learned that fear doesn't mean *stop* – it means *pay attention*. Fear shows you where growth is waiting. When you say yes to what scares you, you reclaim the part of yourself that believes you can't. You remind your body that courage isn't the absence of fear; it's the willingness to move through it.

There's also power in saying no. Saying no is a boundary, a declaration of self-respect. Sometimes saying no to a thought that holds you back is the same as saying yes to the part of you that wants to move forward. Each yes and no carries energy, and how we use them shapes our path. Healing is learning to choose consciously – to say yes to what expands you and no to what shrinks you.

Life will always offer chances to begin again. The mind says, "It's too late," but the heart knows better. Every season invites renewal. The Fall Equinox reminds me of this: the reaping, the harvesting, the gathering of what we've grown. What you planted in the spring and tended through summer is ready to be brought in, digested, integrated. Every ending is simply another beginning.

Harvesting What You've Grown

Every season brings its own invitation to pause and reflect. As fall arrives, I often think about the harvest – the moment when you finally gather what you've sown. Spring is for planting, summer is for tending, and fall is for reaping the lessons and the growth that have been unfolding all along. That rhythm reminds me that there's no such thing as being behind in life. You're always exactly where you're meant to be in your own cycle of growth.

The harvest isn't just about what you've achieved; it's about digesting what life has given you as well. It's about allowing yourself to take in all that you've learned and become because of the journey. When you look back at what you've been through and can finally say, *I grew from that*, you're harvesting. The beauty of it is that you get to enjoy the fruits of your own effort – the insight, the stillness, the acceptance that comes from having walked through it all.

That's what this chapter, and really the whole journey of this book, has been about. Feeling, healing, integrating, and allowing. So as we move towards the final pages, I want to underline the idea again that it's never too late for you to take responsibility for your part in the story. It's never too late to apologize or to offer empathy, to say *I'm sorry* or *I understand*. Every act of ownership brings you closer to freedom. Healing isn't about being perfect; it's about being honest with yourself and others. The more you take responsibility for what's yours, the lighter you become.

Never Too Late to Love

It's also never too late to love yourself. That's one of the greatest truths I've learned. Even when you've believed the lies your mind tells you – that you're too damaged, too old, or too far gone – it's never too late to return to love. Love is always happening, just like time. It doesn't stop; it just waits for your attention. And the moment you choose to soften toward yourself, you begin to feel its presence again.

Love isn't a finish line. It's a practice, a decision you make every day to show up with kindness for the person you are. You are whole and complete as you are – and that's not a slogan; it's a truth that lives in your bones. When you stop fighting who you are, you stop splitting yourself in half. You stop making healing another project to accomplish and instead let it become a way of being.

It's never too late to love others either. That love can show up in the smallest gestures – in the way you listen, the way you smile, even the way you offer light in a dark moment. It's never too late to turn your light back on, even when you've forgotten it was there. The course corrections, the realizations, the moments of humility – they're all just ways of returning to love.

The Gift of Relaxation

When we finally allow ourselves to slow down, we discover how much tension we've been carrying. Stress is one of the biggest time-stoppers there is – it pulls us out of the present and traps us in constant reaction. When you take a breath, even one conscious breath, you return to yourself. You don't have to control time, or the outcome, or anyone else's opinion. You just breathe, and in that breath you find release.

I often guide people through what is called the four-by-four breath: inhale for four counts, hold for four, exhale for four, and hold again for four. It's simple, but it's profound. With every inhale, you invite calm; with every exhale, you let go of what no longer serves you. And when you whisper to yourself, *relax now*, something in your body listens. Your shoulders drop, your mind softens, and the noise quiets just enough for you to hear what's true underneath the stress.

As you keep breathing, your awareness moves through your body. You notice the top of your head, your eyes, your heart, your lungs. You remember that your body is working for you all the time, carrying you through everything you've ever survived. It's a practice that isn't about escaping your feelings; but more about meeting them with tenderness. The more you breathe into your own presence, the more you remember that peace isn't somewhere else – it's right there within you, waiting in the stillness.

Through to the Other Side

There comes a moment when you realize you've made it through – not because everything is fixed or perfect, but because you're no longer fighting yourself. You've stopped judging your emotions and started honoring them. You've stopped trying to think your way out of pain and started feeling your way through it. That's what healing really is. It's the willingness to be real, to show up as you are, to keep choosing yourself *even when it's hard*.

As you look back on your journey through the lessons in these pages, remember where you've walked: You've learned to listen to your emotions instead of running from them, to forgive not because someone deserves it but because you deserve peace. You've learned that boundaries aren't walls – they're invitations to authenticity. You've discovered that stillness isn't the absence of movement but the presence of awareness. You've learned that loving yourself isn't selfish; it's the most healing act there is. Every step, every pause, and every tear has been a part of your unfolding – and it will continue, always.

Because the truth is, growth never ends. There will always be another layer to feel, another part of yourself to meet with compassion. But now you know how. You know that when fear rises, you can breathe. When pain resurfaces, you can stay. When life feels uncertain, you can return to what's real. You have everything you need within you, and you've already proven that you can walk through what once felt impossible.

No matter where you are on your own journey, remember that it's never too late to heal, grow, love and reclaim your own light. In fact, it's what the world needs from you – your brilliance, your sparkle, your unique way of being. When you let yourself shine, you remind others that they can too.

Healing doesn't make you someone new; it helps you remember who you've always been. You are whole and complete as you are, and you hold the power within you to release old pain, rewrite limiting stories, and step into a life of healing, freedom, and authentic self-expression. So keep going. Keep feeling. Keep trusting that the only way out is through. Because it's true – you can't think your way to healing. You have to feel your way through.

Moving Forward

You have just walked through a journey that invited you to feel what you may have spent years trying not to feel. You may have met parts of yourself that were waiting to be witnessed and moved towards coming home to yourself.

As you move forward, remember that this work is not linear. You will return to old emotions, revisit familiar stories, and uncover new layers when you least expect them. That is not a setback. It is the natural rhythm of healing. Every breath, every pause, every moment you choose to feel instead of flee becomes another step toward freedom, clarity, and self-trust.

If this book stirred something inside you, whether a question, a memory, or a pull toward deeper work, know that you do not have to walk the next part alone. Healing becomes steadier and more grounded when you have support. If you feel ready to continue this journey with guidance, reflection, and a safe place to land, I invite you to reach out. If I can do this, so can you. I would be honored to walk beside you as you take your next step.

sharynnichols@feeltoheal.com
https://feeltoheal.com

About Sharyn Nichols

Sharyn is a Licensed Marriage & Family Therapist and Life Guide in Los Angeles, California. With over 25 years of experience in mental health and wellness, she offers a holistic approach drawing from a number of diverse techniques from the yogic traditions, Human Design, and evidence-based strategies such as Cognitive Behavioral Therapy. These practices can help clients experience a heightened awareness of their personal signs of stress and to learn tools to help them challenge negative thoughts. As a certified Kundalini Yoga teacher, she helps clients connect their mind, body, and spirit for a holistic healing experience so that they can learn to connect on their own with their true selves.

Sharyn is warm and compassionate. She creates environments which encourage her clients to feel all their emotions to facilitate the healing process. She skillfully guides her clients to work through feelings of frustration, anger, bitterness, and more to achieve satisfying, peaceful, and successful lives.

As a result of Sharyn's own journey, she has learned to look at life through a different perspective: how to discern what we can control and what we cannot control, and to finally stop living the definition of insanity, i.e. doing the same thing over and over and expecting a different result.

Are you ready to create a more satisfying, peaceful, and successful life for yourself now? Isn't it time to fully feel your feelings, give up the insanity, and finally heal yourself?

sharynnichols1@gmail.com
https://feeltoheal.com

About the Editor

As the editor behind Podcast to Bookshelf, Kim Dietrich helps visionary entrepreneurs and thought leaders transform their spoken words into timeless books that amplify their voices and expand their reach. Kim's editorial eye is intuitive and exacting; she brings clarity, flow, and heart to every manuscript she shapes. As Editorial Director for ICN Publishing, Kim oversees all written content, while helping to guide the creative vision. In her own business she also supports authors and entrepreneurs in bringing their stories to life with authenticity and impact.

kim@kimdietrich.ca
https://yourbookyourway.kimdietrich.ca/